*As an Arizona native of Mexican and indigenous roots, Torres's writings help me orientate myself within the birthright of my Sonoran heritage. This collection is a vital reminder that brown communities built the culture of Southern Arizona from corazón and tradition.*

Marc David Pinate, Producing Director for Borderlands Theatre

*This powerful preservation of Alva Torres's column honors the generations of our gente who treasured their Tucson homes, their traditional foods, their interwoven families, and a community's enduring faith. Each column demonstrates how our cultural and local past is every bit as important today as it was when these were first printed. Through her intimate and relational style, Torres warmly invites us to remember Tucson's own voice.*

Melani "Mele" Martinez, Tucson Writer and Flamenco Artist

*Alva B. Torres's columns were an amazing gift to this city at a time when Tucson was struggling to recover some of itself erased by federal urban renewal activities. I have no doubt that her words—and her community leadership—were paramount in helping us to more ferociously embrace our cultural strengths and to create a greater awareness of the importance of historical preservation.*

Dianne M. Bret Harte, Former Executive Director at the Southwestern Foundation for Education and Historical Preservation

*We need more local books such as Notitas to help document the larger Latinx experience. First-hand accounts like those included here are important resources for understanding the past.*

Desiree Aranda, Co-Chair of Latinos in Heritage Conservation

*Although busy in the first few years out of law school, I always looked for Alva Torres's columns. They brought me back to a simpler time of my grandmother and my mother's stories. Great memories of our connections to each other and our prior generations.*

Margarita B. Bernal, Former Municipal Court Judge

*If you care about where you live—and you should—this collection will add richness to your daily experience and root your life in a deeper Tucson story.*

Aengus Anderson, Oral Historian for the University of Arizona Libraries

*Notitas provides the opportunity to read Alva B. Torres's words and learn more about the columnist, her love for Tucson and the history of nuestra gente.*

Betty Villegas, Director of the Mexican American Museum

*Notitas is a must-read for individuals interested in women's voices, Tucson history, and public history. In this book of columns compiled by Lydia Otero, Torres provides us an invitation to know her Tucson, her neighbors, her experiences. She presents us with a glimpse into the vibrant Tucson that is rarely found in the history books.*

Ceci Durazo Lewis, Douglas Oral History Project

*Alva B. Torres's columns are near-perfect snapshots of what it is to be a Tucsonense. Reading Notitas was like being given the opportunity to return to my childhood and visit with a favorite tía I hadn't seen in a long time.*

Mauro Trejo, Turquoise Trail Guide

*Notitas invites us to learn more about Alva B. Torres and the issues and moments that inspired her activism.*

Lane Santa Cruz, Tucson Council Member

# Notitas

# *Notitas*

Select Columns From
The *Tucson Citizen,*
1984–1993

### *by* Alva B. Torres

Compiled by Lydia R. Otero

PLANET EARTH PRESS
TUCSON, ARIZONA

**Notitas: Select Columns from the Tucson Citizen by Alva B. Torres**
First Edition
Forward and Compilation © 2021 Lydia R. Otero
"Spring at the Foot of the Black Mountain" © Alva B. Torres
Unless otherwise noted, all columns and recipes © USA TODAY NETWORK
All Rights Reserved
Planet Earth Press
www.planetearthpressaz.com

Available in following format:
ISBN-13: 978-1-7341180-2-5 (Paperback)

Cover design, interior design, and typesetting by Sara Thaxton

Publisher's Cataloging-in-Publication Data

Names: Torres, Alva B., author. | Otero, Lydia R., compiler.
Title: Notitas : select columns from the Tucson Citizen / by Alva B. Torres ; compiled by Lydia R. Otero.
Description: Tucson, AZ: Planet Earth Press, 2021.
Identifiers: LCCN: 2021914736 | ISBN: 978-1-7341180-2-5
Subjects: LCSH Torres, Alva B. | Tucson (Ariz.)—Social life and customs. | Interviews—Arizona—Tucson. | Tucson (Ariz.)—Biography. | Tucson (Ariz.)—Newspapers. | Mexican Americans—Arizona—Tucson. | BISAC BIOGRAPHY & AUTOBIOGRAPHY / Cultural, Ethnic & Regional / Hispanic & Latino | BIOGRAPHY & AUTOBIOGRAPHY / Social Activists | LITERARY COLLECTIONS / Women Authors | LANGUAGE ARTS & DISCIPLINES / Journalism | HISTORY / United States / State & Local / Southwest (AZ, NM, OK, TX)
Classification: LCC F819.T953 T67 2021 | DDC 979.1/776—dc23

*Dedicated to the memory of two inspirational movers and
shakers who loved Tucson and committed so much of their time
and efforts to make it a better and more just city*

## Richard Elías
*(1958–2020)*

*and*

## Ann-Eve Pedersen
*(1965–2021)*

Historians have written that a city exists in space as well as time. However, cities exist because of the love of those rare citizens like yourself who give them dimension and distinction in their time.

—The Tucson Bicentennial Committee to Alva B. Torres

# Contents

# 1990

# 1991

# 1992

# Illustrations

# Forward

From 1984 to 1993, one of Tucson, Arizona's major newspapers, the *Tucson Citizen*, featured a weekly column authored by Alva B. Torres. In the journalistic world, she stands out as one of the first Mexican American women whose weekly column appeared in a newspaper that serviced one of the top fifty most highly populated cities in the United States (U.S.).* Oftentimes, her column appeared nestled between nationally syndicated columnists like Erma Bombeck and Ann Landers.

Tucson's newspapers had included other columnists who wrote in Spanish but Torres appealed to a different readership. Written in English, Torres's columns spoke to the generation of Mexican Americans, born in the U.S., and who had attended schools that prohibited them from speaking Spanish, even on playgrounds, and that taught them to read and write only in English. This included the generation referred to as the "baby boomers," like myself and older generations who had attended regional schools.

Born Alva Bustamante in 1932 in Tucson, she attended local schools and graduated from Tucson High School in 1950. In 1953, she married Arthur A. Torres and they had three children. Although rare for a Mexican American, Alva received a two-year liberal arts degree at the University of Arizona. Even at a young age, she prioritized remaining active in community affairs, organizations and social clubs. Eight years before launching her column, Torres had already made a name for herself, and the Tucson Advertising Club named her 1975's "Woman of the Year" for her efforts in historic preservation

---

*In terms of population, Tucson ranked 45th in the nation in 1980 and moved up to 34th in 2021. Top 100 Biggest US Cities By Population, "Tucson, Arizona Population History," https://www.biggestuscities.com/city/tucson-arizona, accessed April 28, 2021.

and for chairing the Tucson Bicentennial Committee that staged numerous events to celebrate the 200th year in which the city was established.

At home, Torres had learned to cook from the women in her family, most prominently from her maternal grandmother in Mexico, and always indulged this passion. After the unfortunate death of her husband Alberto in June of 1976, she put these skills to work and ran a catering business for a number of years and also served as the director of the Southern Arizona Restaurant Association that focused on organizing restaurants and sharing resources.

I lived in Los Angeles, California during the time Alva wrote her weekly columns, but I returned to Tucson frequently to visit with my mother, Chita. Although she listened to radio in Spanish, Chita preferred books and publications written in English and subscribed to the *Citizen*. Upon my arrival, she shared a pile of Alva's columns that she had clipped during my time away to share with me. As I compiled the columns for this book, I was reminded that Torres's column was the only print media where the names of ordinary folks that my mother may have known or a local business that she frequented may have appeared. A mention of the familiar, in the local paper, however fleeting, was no small matter—and made it clip-worthy for Chita and certainly many others.

Little did I know then, that I would come to call Alva B. Torres a friend and one who continues to inspire me to this day. It was her role in historic preservation that drew my attention as I began the research that culminated in the publication of my book, *La Calle: Spatial Conflicts and Urban Renewal in a Southwest City* in 2010. Before writing her weekly column, Torres had organized the Society for the Preservation of Tucson's Plaza de la Mesilla or La Placita Committee, the most formidable resistance effort to urban renewal that targeted Tucson's oldest barrios in the late 1960s. These few lines from *La Calle* summarize the critical role she played:

Recognizing that urban renewal threatened not only buildings but also memory, Torres initiated a public battle to preserve both a place—a Tucson landmark—and an essential part of Southern Arizona history. At the core of the debate over urban renewal lay conflicting visions of the past Tucsonans wished to celebrate and the future they hoped to construct. The La Placita Committee, consisting mostly of women, emerged to challenge what it saw as the cultural elitism inherent in urban renewal policies. Led and organized by

Torres, this grassroots organization, armed with a heightened historical consciousness, became urban renewal's earliest and most formidable foe.*

Alva continued to advocate for historic preservation and served on what would become the Tucson-Pima County Historic Commission for six years (1974–1980). In this book, I have included several columns that she authored to spread the word about the importance of landmarks such as the Sosa-Carrillo House, El Tiradito, and La Casa de Cordova.[†]

In spite of Alva B. Torres's extensive activism, the newspaper initially offered her the opportunity to write a weekly column based on her culinary skills. When it debuted, the newspaper's editor noted that the new column would provide readers the ". . . secrets to cooking good Mexican food at home." Torres grasped the opportunity to write for the newspaper and named her column, "Recipes and Notitas." A literal English-language translation of *"notitas"* is notes, but it also references shorter stories, which is why I selected it for this book's title. When the column premiered on September 12, 1984, as promised, it focused on recipes, but Torres increasingly began to share childhood memories and to profile family members. She also started to write about other *Tucsonenses*, as many Mexican Americans who live in Tucson like to refer to themselves, and her vast network of friends. Less than one year after its launching, because of the column's popularity and because the writer herself started including more topics, the newspaper dropped the old title affiliated with recipes and referred to the column as simply "Alva B. Torres."

It is worth mentioning that the *Citizen* allowed Torres the freedom to evolve and decide what information made it into her columns. Alva shared with me that she mulled over topics for the column during the week based on the conversations she engaged in, news items, and the events she attended. She timed her arrival at the *Citizen* building on Sunday afternoons when it was empty, used an office computer to write her column for that week and

---

*See *La Calle: Spatial Conflicts and Urban Renewal in a Southwest City* (Tucson: University of Arizona Press, 2010), p. 127.

†More information is available about Torres's activism at the Arizona Historical Society/Tucson, MS 1134, Alva Torres Collection. Also see my entry "Alva B. Torres," in Vicki Ruíz and Virginia Sánchez Korrol, eds., *Latinas in the United States a Historical Encyclopedia* (Bloomington: Indiana University Press, 2006), 756–757.

left a copy for editing. The newspaper never refused to publish one of her columns.

Notable families who had lived in Tucson for generations were often mentioned in Torres's columns, as were individuals active in local school programs, civic life, or who had started businesses. She also profiled buildings and the places important to Tucsonenses and their collective cultural practices and beliefs. An early proponent of immigration rights, she used a few of her columns to discuss her involvement with the U.S. Immigration and Control Act of 1986. Employed by the Diocese of Tucson, Torres coordinated efforts to encourage undocumented residents, who arrived before 1982, to engage in and pursue their U.S. citizenship before the expiration of the amnesty deadline.

Each column in this book provides an opportunity to learn about Alva B. Torres as a person and about her life. We also learn about her social world and times. Some columns provide insight into the strong attachment to traditional gender roles and the limitations of language such as referring to a woman who led organizations as the "chairman." We also see how the ethnic identifier "Hispanic" starts to take hold in the journalistic world in the late 1980s and how even Torres starts using this term.

Despite taking a sabbatical between 1987 and 1988, Torres wrote 362 columns for the *Citizen*. I reviewed all of them and immersed myself in a series of difficult decisions to determine which columns to include in this book compilation. I organized them chronologically and hesitated changing a word or revising a sentence. Over time, Torres's columns became longer and sometimes focused on multiple topics. Because of this, I shortened some columns to either fit onto a printed page or to highlight a single issue. Alva has previously published a book of recipes, and thus I did not include many in this compilation.* The few included demonstrate a distinctive local connection. They evidence a knowledge that came from decades of living in Southern Arizona and accentuate local flavors and preferences.

---

*A copy of this book of recipes is available at Special Collections at the University of Arizona. See Alba B. Torres, *Recipes y Notitas: Healthy Mexican Cooking* (Tucson: Old Pueblo Printers, 1997). Torres often called herself Alba when in the company of close friends and relatives.

FIGURE F.1  Front cover of Alva Torres's 1997 book.

The payment Torres received for each column was minimal, and although she knew other columnists were making much more, she continued to write her weekly column. Since the newspaper paid Alva for her services, the *Citizen* legally owned the columns and I needed to acquire permission and pay a licensing fee for each one I reprinted in this book. To make a long story of corporate acquisitions short, USA Today now legally owns Alva B. Torres's columns. Thus, I am thankful for the Southwestern Foundation for Education and Historical Preservation's generosity and willingness to make this book a reality by covering the licensing fees. Ann-Eve Pedersen, the organization's former executive director, played a critical role in the initial stages when I was formulating this book of columns, and I will forever appreciate her excitement, encouragement and support.

I spent the time sequestered and adhering to COVID-19 precautions compiling this book. Rarely did the columns published in the newspaper include a photograph. Those included in this book were added to provide context or enhance a subject referenced in a Torres column. With the exception of advertisemento and announcements, none of the photographs in this book appeared in newspaper.

I found that the topics and issues that Alva Torres discussed in her columns remain salient, and I consider each one as providing a single frame of information that when read together provides a dynamic diorama about the practices and aspirations of an evolving people and city. Over time, I came

FIGURE F.2 Alva B. Torres and Lydia Otero in 2004 at an event commem orating the 150th anniversary of the signing of El Tratado de la Mesilla or Gadsden Treaty that made Southern Arizona a part of the United States. Lydia R. Otero Collection.

to appreciate how Torres's columns speak to how Tucsonenses maintained a sense of themselves and community whether through events or shared memories during 1984–1993. Although never overtly political, through her column, Torres continually reminded her readers that Mexican people and culture had always played a critical role in Tucson's past and in its present. I appreciate this perspective and am grateful to have participated in making this book a reality.

Lydia R. Otero
June 5, 2021
Tucson, Arizona

*Notitas*

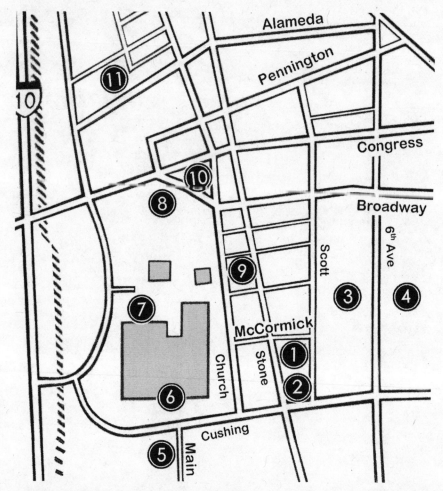

# DOWNTOWN SITES OFTEN MENTIONED BY ALVA B. TORRES

1. Childhood Home @ 35 East McCormick Street
2. The Temple of Music and Art @ 330 South Scott Avenue
3. The Downtown Carnegie Library @ 200 South 6th Avenue
4. Armory Park @ 220 South 5th Avenue
5. El Tiradito @ 420 South Main Avenue
6. The Tucson Convention Center @ 260 South Church Avenue
7. The Sosa-Carrillo (Fremont) House @ 151 South Granada Avenue
8. The Kiosko (Bandshell) in La Placita @ 73–199 West Broadway Boulevard
9. Cathedral of Saint Augustine @ 192 South Stone Avenue
10. Veinte de Agosto Park and Francisco "Pancho" Villa Statue @ 105 West Congress Street
11. La Casa Cordova and the Tucson Museum of Art @ 175 North Meyer Avenue

# 1984

# New cooking column gives some hints on preparing chiles

*Editor's note: This marks the beginning of a weekly column in Focus on the secrets to cooking good Mexican food at home. Columnist Alva B. Torres, a native Tucsonan, will sprinkle her column with anecdotes on Mexican heritage.*

She was born in the Stork's Nest, a maternity hospital downtown, in 1932. As a child, she learned how to cook from her grandmother.

She has been executive director of the Southern Arizona Restaurant Association and runs a catering business from Alberto's Mexican Restaurant, 1118 W. St. Mary's Road.

The mother of two sons and a daughter, Torres has been one of Tucson's leading civic volunteers, working for the preservation of Tucson's heritage. She was honored in 1976 as Tucson's Woman of the Year by the Tucson Advertising Club. Recently, she has been planning a fund-raising fair for St. Elizabeth's of Hungary Clinic.

**Recipes and notitas**
By Alva B. Torres

**By ALVA B. TORRES**
For the Tucson Citizen

Few things in the world are as universally enjoyed and shared as eating the food we have prepared.

Yet the same dish may have as many different recipes as it has cooks. For example, tacos may have countless tastes depending on who cooks them.

This column will deal with recipes, mostly for Mexican dishes, from Tucson and the regions of Mexico with which I am familiar. I'll also write about recipes from homemakers, caterers and restaurateurs in the Tucson area.

I learned my love of cooking when I was a very little girl from my grandmother who was from Sinaloa. She is in my mind as I write.

Many of the foods we enjoy in Tucson originally came from Sonora, our neighboring Mexican state, as well as from Sinaloa, further south. A few of our favorite dishes seem to have originated right here in Tucson and I intend to tell you about them.

If there is a particular dish or ingredient that interests you, or a special recipe you would like, let me know so that I can try to include it in a column.

This first column will not have a recipe. Instead, I want to give you time to prepare for next week's recipe for *chiles rellenos* (long green chiles stuffed with cheese). It takes time to track down the right ingredients.

Fresh chiles are available through the summer at a fair price, so this is the time to purchase them. The recipe will be geared to right chiles. You will also need oregano, four eggs, a half-pound of longhorn cheese, one whole medium onion, one 4-ounce can of tomato sauce and vinegar. I prefer a good white or red wine vinegar.

Green chiles freeze well. I usually roast them as soon as possible after I get them home. You can do this either on your stove top or in the broiler. On a gas stove, you can place the chiles directly on the grid over the flame. On an electric stove, you must roast them on a metal griddle or in a heavy skillet. To roast them in the broiler, they should be 2 inches from the flame. All methods require that you turn the chiles often to prevent them from burning.

When the skin on the chiles blisters and begins to pull away from the flesh, remove them from the source of heat. Place them in a regular paper bag and close it. The steam in the bag will make the chiles easier to peel. Do not remove the stem when peeling. The stem indicates that you are an authentic cook and have used fresh rather than canned green chiles.

Cut the chiles by slitting them along the length and scrape out the seeds. Then rinse them and place them in plastic bag, eight to a bag. Pop them in the freezer, so that when you want *chiles rellenos*, they are ready.

If you can plan ahead, take the chiles out of the freezer the night before and place them, frozen, in a shallow rectangular glass container. Cover them, just barely, with water and add about a half-tablespoon of wine vinegar. Let them stand, covered with plastic wrap, overnight. Do not discard the vinegar-water. You will used it later in the recipe. Next week, I will give you the basic recipe and a variation, which comes from Sinaloa. You can make it your main dish — an unforgettably delicious one.

Cariñosamente

*Questions and letters may be addressed to Alva B Torres, 334 S. Sixth Ave., Tucson, Az 85701. If you need a reply, please enclose a stamped, self-addressed envelope.*

FIGURE 1.1 Inaugural column. *Citizen*, September 12, 1984, p. 1B.

# New Cooking Column Gives Some Hints on Preparing Chiles

*Citizen Editor's note: This marks the beginning of a weekly column in Focus [a section of the newspaper] on the secrets to cooking good Mexican food at home. Columnist Alva B. Torres, a native Tucsonan, will sprinkle her column with anecdotes on Mexican heritage. She was born in the Stork's Nest, a maternity hospital downtown, in 1932. As a child, she learned how to cook from her grandmother.*

*She has been executive director of the Southern Arizona Restaurant Association and runs a catering business from Alberto's Mexican Restaurant, 1118 W. St. Mary's Road. The mother of two sons and a daughter, Torres has been one of Tucson's leading civic volunteers, working for the preservation of Tucson's heritage. She was honored in 1976 as Tucson's Woman of the Year by the Tucson Advertising Club. Recently, she has been planning a fund-raising fair for St. Elizabeth's of Hungary Clinic.*

\* \* \*

## By ALVA B. TORRES
For the Tucson Citizen

Few things in the world are as universally enjoyed and shared as eating the food we have prepared. Yet the same dish may have as many different recipes as it has cooks. For example, tacos may have countless tastes depending on who cooks them.

This column will deal with recipes, mostly for Mexican dishes, from Tucson and the regions of Mexico with which I am familiar. I'll also write about recipes from homemakers, caterers and restaurateurs in the Tucson area.

I learned my love of cooking when I was a very little girl from my grandmother who was from Sinaloa. She is in my mind as I write.

Many of the foods we enjoy in Tucson originally came from Sonora, our neighboring Mexican state, as well as from Sinaloa, further south. A few of our favorite dishes seem to have originated right here in Tucson and I intend to tell you about them.

If there is a particular dish or ingredient that interests you, or a special recipe you would like, let me know so that I can try to include it in a column.

This first column will not have a recipe. Instead, I want to give you time to prepare for next week's recipe for *chiles rellenos** (long green chiles stuffed with cheese). It takes time to track down the right ingredients.

Fresh chiles are available through the summer at a fair price, so this is the time to purchase them. The recipe will be geared to eight chiles. You will also need oregano, four eggs, a half-pound of longhorn cheese, one whole medium onion, one 4-ounce can of tomato sauce and vinegar. I prefer a good white or red wine vinegar.

Green chiles freeze well. I usually roast them as soon as possible after I get them home. You can do this either on your stove top or in the broiler. On a gas stove, you can place the chiles directly on the grid over the flame. On an electric stove, you must roast them on a metal griddle or in a heavy skillet. To roast them in the broiler, they should be 2 inches from the flame. All methods require that you turn the chiles often to prevent them from burning.

When the skin on the chiles blisters and begins to pull away from the flesh, remove them from the source of heat. Place them in a regular paper bag and close it. The steam in the bag will make the chiles easier to peel. Do not remove the stem when peeling. The stem indicates that you are an authentic cook and have used fresh rather than canned green chiles.

Cut the chiles by slitting them along the length and scrape out the seeds. Then rinse them and place them in plastic bag, eight to a bag. Pop them in the freezer, so that when you want chiles rellenos, they are ready.

If you can plan ahead, take the chiles out of the freezer the night before and place them, frozen, in a shallow rectangular glass container. Cover them,

---

*Words borrowed from the Spanish language will only be italicized if that is how they appeared in the newspaper.

just barely, with water and add about a half-tablespoon of wine vinegar. Let them stand, covered with plastic wrap, overnight. Do not discard the vinegar-water. You will used it later in the recipe. Next week, I will give you the basic recipe and a variation, which comes from Sinaloa. You can make it your main dish—an unforgettably delicious one.

  *Cariñosamente.*

* * *

*Questions and letters may be addressed to Alva B. Torres, 334 S. Sixth Avenue, Tucson, Az. 85701. If you need a reply, please enclose a stamped, self-addressed envelope.*

# As Promised, Here's My Recipe for *Chiles Rellenos*

In my column last week, I told you what ingredients to have ready to make *chiles rellenos*. Today I will give you the recipe I learned from a faithful old friend of my grandmother when I was very young.

Although I offer you the recipe my family likes, when you are making the sauce of tomatoes and oregano, you should taste it. Make it your individual dish by adding any other herb that suits you, or by controlling the consistency of the sauce with more water, more tomato or even stock. You can always add a little more oregano or vinegar, too. This is what makes cooking so universal and yet unique.

Choose either longhorn cheese or a white cheese that melts well, such as Monterey Jack. I usually take two days to prepare this dish, roasting and preparing the chiles and marinating them overnight. But you can do it in one afternoon if you wish, marinating them for just a few hours.

### *CHILES RELLENOS*

4 large eggs
8 fresh green chiles
½ pounds of longhorn or other white cheese
1 medium white onion, thinly sliced
1 clove of garlic, minced
1 teaspoon of dried oregano
4-ounce can of tomato sauce
½ tablespoon of wine vinegar
1½ cups of water
1½ cup of vegetable oil

1. Roast and peel the chiles and remove the seeds. Place them in a glass bowl that contains enough water to cover the chiles, along with tablespoon of wine vinegar. Let the chiles sit overnight or for a few hours, covered. Do not discard the vinegar-water.

2. Separate the eggs. Beat the egg whites. If you wish, add a pinch of cream of tartar. (At this point, half the world adds a little flour. You may if you like. I do not.) Add the yolks after the whites hold a peak and fold them in gently.

3. Remove the chiles from the marinade. Cut the cheese in slices and place one piece inside each chile. Slice the onion and peel and mince the garlic. Okay, now you are ready to go.

4. Place a heavy skillet (cast iron is best) on the fire and heat the pan until water sprinkled on it jumps up. Meanwhile set the stuffed chilies next to the pan and set your spatula within easy reach. Set the beaten eggs next to this, as close as possible to the chiles. As soon as the pan is ready, add the cup of oil.

5. When it is heated take the first chili by the stem and the tail and immerse it in the egg batter, then place it gently in the hot oil. With the spatula push the oil around the chili. Using the stem and the spatula, turn it over and push it to one side. Continue this until all eight chiles are fried. (If you need more oil, use it.) Remove them from the pan and drain on paper toweling.

6. Now take the sliced onion and sauté it until it is wilted. Add the garlic and sauté it lightly. Add the oregano and the tomato sauce to the pan, along with the reserved vinegar-water. Add the fried chiles. If necessary, add more water, enough to cover the chiles. Add salt to suit. Taste it. Gently simmer until heated through.

# La Llorona, Halloween and Pumpkin Tea

How do you coax children into coming home in the evening when it gets dark? Four centuries ago in Mexico, they used a legend. La Llorona, the wailing woman or weeping woman, is a fascinating tale that dates to seventeenth-century Mexico. Frances Gillmor, a retired University of Arizona professor, helped me pin down the origin of La Llorona.

The legend, used in small towns in Mexico and the Southwest, was aimed at frightening children into getting home before dark, lest they would be snatched by the despairing, ever yearning, weeping mother, to hold as her own children. The two main legends that I am familiar with both involve a woman in a trauma. They also involve her little ones and water. I suppose with flash floods being so treacherous and sudden, it was vital for children to get home before dark.

Anyway, in one version, this young wife supposedly finds out that her husband is unfaithful, and in a fit of rage, she drowns their children, in order to make him feel as terrible as she feels. When she realizes what she has done, she goes into a panic and begins to look for them, and continues to do so constantly. She can be heard wailing in the dark night, with desolate cries, begging for her little ones.

The second version is that of a young, poverty-stricken widow who cannot feed her children. Rather than see them starve, she decides that she is going to throw them into a swirling arroyo and then jump in herself. She throws them in and when she is about to leap in, she becomes totally terrified at what she has just done. She falls on her knees and begins pleading for them to return. She goes home and puts on a black *tapalo* (shawl), as she is in deep mourning already for her deceased husband and is dressed completely in black. Because of her tapalo, no one ever has seen her face. More often, she is described not so much as evil, but as one out of her mind with grief, ever condemned to walk the earth after dark, while searching for her lost children.

There is a melancholy song, "Llorona." Part of the lyrics say, "Tapáme con tu rebozo, Llorona, porque me muero de frio." (Cover me with your shawl, weeper, because I die of cold.) Cold in poetry can mean cold or it can mean unrequited love.

So much for legends. Something good to make for this evening is té de calabaza (pumpkin tea).

It is smooth and delicate and a definite treat.

## TE DE CALABAZA

1 quart of water

3-ounce package of cinnamon sticks

1 cone of *panocha* (Mexican brown sugar cone) or 3 ounces sugar

½ cup of raisins and prunes (optional)

2 cups of chopped uncooked pumpkin

3 tea bags

1. Bring all ingredients to a boil, except tea.

2. Lower to a simmer for an hour then bring to a boil once more and pour over the tea.

3. Cool and serve warm.

In Mexico, this is served with a little lime juice and sugar to taste. They also use small sugarcane swizzle sticks. I hope you have a spooky and safe Halloween.

# Happy Tradition: Christmas Tamales

Congratulations to Livia "Lilly" Montiel for taking first prize in the tamale division at the recent Fiesta for St. Elizabeth of Hungary Clinic.* Also, a big "thank you" to all of you who supported the event.

Let's get on with the recipe for tamales, as promised. They are a special part of Christmas celebrations in Southern Arizona and Northern Mexico. Curiously, they are normally not eaten on Christmas Day in every part of Mexico.

The following recipe from Lilly Montiel yields two dozen tamales and uses the traditional lard along with the meat and red chili sauce to fill the dried corn husks. Some people nowadays use a vegetable shortening in place of the lard. Also, many stores feature cuts of beef they label "for tamale making." If you don't see it, ask the butcher.

Two dozen isn't very many tamales. But making a small amount like this, particularly for a novice, is a good idea because if anything is amiss you won't be afraid to try again. And if they turn out delicious, you will have to! So, nothing but winners can result.

If you make larger amounts, make it easy on yourself and cook the *chile colorado* (red chili sauce), the day before. Also, if you can cook and cut up the pork and the beef beforehand, it will help. If you want to make it a lot of fun, have a *tamalada*. That is a tamale-making party and is traditional in this part of the country. In the olden days the beating of the lard and *masa* [ground nixtamalized corn] was done by the papá or the women with the strongest arms. Everything was done with the whole family and friends and cooked on Christmas Eve. Some families would leave the tamales cooking while they

---

*Established at 140 West Speedway Boulevard in 1961, in a time of limited health services, St. Elizabeth of Hungary was one of the few clinics that provided health and dental care services for those with lower incomes in Southern Arizona.

went to midnight Mass and then eat the tamales while they opened their gifts. No matter how you do it, if you follow directions, you are in for a treat.

## LILLY MONTIEL'S TAMALES*

3 cups of chile colorado

1⅓ pounds of beef for tamales

⅔ pounds of pork

3 garlic cloves

1 rib celery, chopped

2½ pounds prepared masa

(*Masa available at many stores listed under Mexican foods in the yellow pages*)

1 pound of lard

1½ teaspoons of salt

¼ pound hojas, or corn husks

1. Place the meats in a kettle and cover with water. Add the garlic and the celery and salt to taste. Bring to a boil, cover, then reduce heat and simmer until tender, about 40 minutes. Allow to cool. Important: Save at least 1 cup of the broth.

2. When the meat is cool enough to handle, cut it into ½ inch dice or smaller. (May be covered and refrigerated at this time.)

3. Heat the diced meat in the 3 cups chile colorado thoroughly (or red chile sauce, homemade or otherwise), by simmering gently so that the favors blend.

4. Now for the masa. With an electric mixer, whip the lard to whipped cream state. Add the masa and continue beating until thoroughly mixed. Add the broth and 1½ teaspoons of salt and continue to beat. The masa is a *punto*, or perfect to the dot, when a pinch of it, dropped into a glass of cool water, rises to the top of the water.

4. Rinse the hojas, or corn husks, and then drain them, but keep them damp. Assemble the meat mixture, the masa mixture and the hojas on a table or counter top. Have a plastic dish rack nearby.

---

*Livia "Lilly" Montiel's recipes are available in a cookbook at the University of Arizona Library's Special Collections. See Patricia Montiel Overall, *Comidas Sabrosas and Other Gourmet Delights: A Century of Favorite Family Recipes* (Tucson, Arizona: P. Overall, 1987).

5. Take a corn husk and open it in the palm of your hand. The wider part of the husk should be at the bottom. The smooth side of the husk should face you. Take three or four level tablespoonfuls, or the equivalent, of masa and spread it onto the husk, ¼-inch thick, on the lower ⅔ of the hoja, not quite to the side edges.

6. Take another spoon and scoop up about two tablespoonfuls of the cooked meat and red chili mixture and place it in the middle of husk that has been coated with the masa.

7. Now, to fold it correctly, you should fold the left side of the husk (masa and all) over onto the middle of the filling. The right side is then folded over the left side snugly. Now fold the top down to make the bundle secure.

8. Do this with the rest of the husks, standing them up like little soldiers (open side up, naturally) in the dish rack.

9. When they are all formed, place the tamales in a steamer with enough water to gently steam them. If you don't have a steamer, improvise with aluminum foil. Just be sure that the tamales do not sit in the water.

10. Cover the pot and bring to a boil. Lower the heat, but keep the steam coming. Steam the tamales for 45 minutes. To test, remove one tamale and let it cool enough to taste. Open the husk and check to see that the dough (or masa) holds together and that there are no white spots on the hojas. Overcooking won't hurt them, so don't worry. Keep enough water in the bottom of the pan so that the steam is continuous.

If you make the tamales ahead of time, they can be frozen before steaming. They can be cooked while frozen, but of course it will take longer than 45 minutes to cook them. However, even after steaming, they keep wonderfully well in the refrigerator for several days.

This is Lilly's recipe. But many people add a little extra chile colorado salsa to the masa for coloring. Also, at Christmas Lilly adds one whole, unpitted green olive to each tamale and a long slice of jalapeño.

A favorite way to eat them is for breakfast. You heat the tamales in a broiler, still in their husks until crispy, then unwrap them and top them with over-easy eggs. These are called tamales *montados*, or mounted, like on a horse.

# 1985

# Mexican Chocolate for a New Pueblo

Today's recipe is an old one (as we say, "oldie but goodie") and is very easy.

It is a Mexican *chocolate* or chocolate—spelled the same way in both Spanish and English. It is pronounced differently, however, with four syllables and the accent on the second to the last one in Spanish.

First, here is the terminology:

*Leche* is milk. *Canela* is cinnamon. *Harina* is flour. *Panocha* is Mexican brown sugar. *Agua* is water.

This recipe makes 10 cups of *champurro* or Mexican hot chocolate.* You can control the sweetness by adding more or less panocha. You can make it more chocolate-y by adding more cocoa, and the thickness is controlled by the amount of flour you use.

### CHAMPURRO

    1 cup of harina (flour)
    8 cups of leche (milk)
    2 large canela (cinnamon) sticks
    4 tablespoons of melted panocha
    4 tablespoons of cocoa
    2 cups of agua (water)
    2 circles of Ibarra Chocolate

Ibarra Chocolate is found in many Mexican specialty stores, supermarkets or in Nogales (in Sonora, Mexico). It contains sugar, cocoa, almonds, cinnamon and lecithin, all ground and pressed into circles, squares or bars.

## Focus

FAN MAIL — Alva Torres, the Tucson Citizen's food columnist and specialist on Mexican cooking, has been flooded with letters from fans. She answers some of them and throws in a recipe, too. **Page 3B.**

FIGURE 2.1 Front page announcement. *Citizen*, January 9, 1985, p.1.

---

*Some may know another version of this beverage as champurrado made with corn flour.

1. Brown the flour in a heavy skillet, and stir it so it will not burn. Make it nice and brown. Set it aside.

2. Simmer the milk, canela sticks, panocha, and cocoa gently for at least thirty minutes.

3. Blend browned flour with water and Ibarra chocolate. Add this to the milk mixture. Simmer it for another 20 minutes or so and serve.

## Notita (Note)

I hope many of you found the [*Citizen*] series, "New Pueblo—Tucson Faces Its Future," interesting, invigorating and motivating. Certainly, being a native Tucsonan, or *Tucsonense*, this series made me more aware than ever of the importance of facing the future challenges now. It does not matter how big Tucson gets; we still can preserve the spirit that it has had since it began.

From everything I know about our history, Tucson always has been *simpatico*. This means arousing a sympathetic response. We always have been a caring people. Many people think of a specific town as a man or a woman. I suppose Chicago would be a man. To me, Tucson is neither. It is a family. The grandparents, or *abuelitos*, are the old historic districts downtown. The children are the four main sections of north, south, east and west. The grand-

FIGURE 2.2  Advertisement. *Citizen*, January 11, 1985, p. 7G.

children are all the outlying areas. The reason things have been difficult to resolve, especially in the times since World War II, is that many people have not understood this. In order to solve our problems, we must first understand the total, and how it affects each segment.

This series is an excellent source of information. If you missed it, it is worth your effort to get a copy. Maybe we cannot map or chart the course for the whole world, but if each couple, each family, each town or city does not seek solutions with those people and places where our own lives are affected on a daily basis, how can we hope for survival of any kind?

I have spent a good part of my life being involved, and yet there is never enough time to realize all the aspects of any one area. I hear people say they waste so much time. Well, we all choose. Each of us has the same 24 hours a day—no more, no less. I don't care if you were here in the "prehistoric" days, as were some of my ancestors, or if you are coming to Tucson soon and only read our newspapers.

As a native, I say, "Welcome." We all get the Tucson that each of us individually and collectively strives toward, day by day.

# Mexican Food 'Too Spicy'? Try *Cocido*

If you are lucky enough to have company and they are not acquainted with Mexican food and probably would rather not taste it, because it is "too spicy," have them try *cocido*.

Cocido simply means cooked or boiled. It is also another word for Spanish stew. But I imagine the Indians on this continent were cooking it long before Cortez arrived in 1519. The cocido we eat now is a blend of the best of all worlds. You can guess which cultures contributed specific ingredients,

My very first column told all of you that I would give you the secrets to cooking good Mexican food at home. One of the secrets to delicious cocido is to use fresh vegetables only, because they are what give the broth its delicate flavor. The other secret is to add the vegetables at the right time, so they don't cook too long or too little.

Guidelines are that you cook the brisket for one hour per pound of meat. The chickpeas take about two to three hours, depending on their age and whether they were soaked or not.

The cocido I make takes a total of four hours.

I have to count backward, then, to know when to add each kind of vegetable. I do it this way:

Green beans and carrots: Four hours minus 15 minutes.
Zucchini: Four hours minus 10 minutes.
During the last six to eight minutes, I add the corn.
Finally, I add the cabbage, about five minutes before zero.

Never, never use chiles or peppers of any kind. If you are making true cocido, I recommend you eat the soup without adding salsa, so that you can savor the fresh vegetable flavors. Some people eat the meat separately, and that is when they might use salsa, horseradish or mustard. Good cuts of meat, naturally, enhance this dish.

Tucsonan Virginia Laos, *una buena cocinera*, serves all the components separately. The beef goes on a meat platter; the large vegetables go on a dish, and the soup, or *caldo*, goes in a tureen (deep soup dish with a cover). She ladles the soup into each of her guests' soup plates, along with the small vegetables, the string beans and chickpeas. The guests serve the rest to themselves.

Another version calls for cooking the chickpeas first separately and then putting everything into the pot at once and cooking it until the meat is tender. My second son says he likes it that way. This soup, along with a good bread or tortillas, makes a good meal in itself.

Many restaurants serve *cocido*. The one most widely known in Tucson for cocido is Micha's restaurant, 2908 South Fourth Avenue. Micha serves it only at noon, because she refuses to reheat it for serving at dinner.*

Cocido is an excellent choice with which to introduce not only guests to Mexican cooking, but for novice cooks to start out with as well, because it is so simple. You will need the following ingredients, varying the amounts of certain of them according to your personal choice. The amounts listed here are merely guidelines:

## COCIDO

2 gallons of water
4 pounds of beef brisket
1 cup of chickpeas
1 head of garlic
1 onion
3 or 4 sweet potatoes
2 or 3 potatoes
½ pound of string beans
1 pound of carrots
½ pound of zucchini

---

*Many restaurants mentioned by Torres have closed their doors. It is improbable that the handful of restaurants such as Micha's, El Charro and others that have survived have the same menus, dishes and specialties that they served more thirty years ago.

3 ears of corn

½ head of cabbage

1. Soak the dry chickpeas overnight. Drain and discard the water.

2. Place the 2 gallons of water into a large pot. Add the beef, drained chickpeas, the whole head of garlic and the whole onion to the pot. (I use my tamale pot.)

3. Bring to a boil, then lower the flame to medium, so that the water is just perking [starting to boil].

4. When meat is tender, after about 3½ hours, peel and slice into circles the sweet potatoes and add them to the pot.

5. Then peel and quarter the white potatoes and add them.

6. Prepare the string beans, cut the carrots in half, and add them to the pot after the pot has come back to a simmer.

7. Slice the zucchini diagonally into thirds and add it.

8. Break the ears of corn into thirds and add them.

9. At about 3 hours and 55 minutes into the cooking time, cut the cabbage into large pieces and add that.

10. Bring the mixture to a simmer once more, cook it for five minutes, and then serve it.

# *Capirotada* is a Great Dessert for Lent

One of Tucson's restaurants serves a unique dessert only during Lent. The restaurant is El Charro. The dessert is *capirotada*, a bread pudding with a little bit of everything, including brown sugar (*panocha*), of course, but also including the unlikely ingredients of white cheese, cilantro and green onion.

El Charro is at 311 North Court Avenue, in the historic El Presidio District. It was established in 1922 by Monica Flin, the daughter of a Frenchman who fashioned the rose window in the old San Agustín Cathedral. The window now graces Arizona History Museum, at 949 East Second Street.

El Charro changed its location during the years, but it is the oldest continuous family-owned restaurant in this area. For the first several years, it was called El Caballero, which meant cavaliers in colonial times. In 1927, Monica changed the name to El Charro, which in Mexico denotes a cavalier, a gentleman horseman. Her great niece, Carlotta Dunn Flores and her husband, Ray, took over the business when it moved from its best-known location on West Broadway during the urban renewal era of the 1960s. Special Lenten meals are served there on Fridays during Lent.

Another family also has been involved almost from the beginning. Mercy Tapia went to work for Monica when she was 13 years old, and she became Monica's lifelong companion, as well as chief cook. Mercy used to grind the corn by hand on the *metate* (grinding stone) to make the *masa* for the tamales. She also made the red chili sauce used for a variety of dishes, including the flat Sonorenese-style enchiladas. These, as well as the *carne seca*, are still made in house by Dora T. Alvarez, Mercy's niece. Dora is now the head cook. She keeps up the good tradition of preparing food as it is ordered by the customers, and she uses fresh products.

FIGURE 2.3  El Charro Restaurant, located in La Placita at 140 West Broadway. Monica Flinn, the restaurant's owner is on the right in this photo taken in the 1960s. Lydia R. Otero Collection.

When my sisters, Julieta and Estherita, and I were little, we walked over to El Charro for dinner, with or without our parents. My mother didn't cook on Sundays, because of a strong religious conviction. We would order No. 1—if our parents gave us the 45 cents—and enjoy tacos and all the trimmings.

At the time, Monica had her own private dining room, where she often entertained family and guests and often cooked her delicious quail and other gourmet dishes. Mercy also was known for her *almendrado*, an egg and almond cream dessert, still served daily. And Dora also has kept up the tradition of inventing new dishes with the Lent-only capirotada.

Here's is Dora's recipe, cut down for home use:

CAPIROTADA
    ½ bunch of fresh cilantro
    ½ bunch of green onions
    6 cups of water
    6 panocha cones

2 to 3 cinnamon sticks

1½ pounds Italian bread

⅓ to ½ pounds grated Jack cheese

½ stick of butter

1 to 2 tablespoons peanuts (optional)

1. Tie the bunches of cilantro (or coriander) and green onions together.

2. Place the bundle in a pot with the water, panocha and cinnamon sticks and boil until the panocha dissolves.

3. Strain through a colander. Make sure to reserve liquid.

4. Cut bread into medium size slices and toast in the oven.

5. Place half of the toasted bread in a 13-inch-by-11-inch-by-2½-inch baking pan.

6. Pour half of the reserved liquid over this and dot with half the butter and half the grated cheese.

7. Repeat with the second half of the ingredients.

8. Cover with foil and place in the oven at 350 degrees until the cheese melts—at least 20 minutes.

9. Serve warm with a dollop of whipped cream.

# Home-cooked Tortillas' Aroma is Indescribable

Ahh . . . that wonderful aroma. You might be smelling tortillas cooking on a wood-burning stove outdoors. To get a whiff of that marvelous smell, go to a tortilla factory. There are some things that cannot be described accurately— they must be experienced.

If you want to get more than a whiff, though, try today's recipe. It is especially nice to make tortillas outdoors. If you have a barbecue pit, you can place a *comal* (a heavy, round, flat iron skillet), or any cooking skillet that resembles a comal over glowing charcoal, mesquite or whatever wood is available.

You can make tortillas on your stove indoors, too, which is where many a good tortilla has been cooked, on either the built-in griddle or if necessary, a heavy, flat griddle, such as those used to make pancakes.

When Cruzita, my *amiga*, makes tortillas, she does not fool around. By 4 a.m., she is *amasando* (kneading) and by 5 a.m., she has her fire going with a mixture of *lena de fierro* (firewood) and mesquite. She claims she can control her fire exactly the way she wants to, by using both types of wood.

She was born almost 75 years ago in a little *ranchito*-like town called San Pedro de la Cueva. It is near Hermosillo in the state of Sonora, Mexico, just south of Arizona. Although she has lived in Tucson for most of her adult life, she still recreates a part of her ranchito here. She has a three-sided shed where she keeps her working table, her wood, her utensils and her towels—all the things she needs for cooking tortillas. Close by, she has her outside wood-burning appliance, where she sets her comal.

At the same time that she makes tortillas, she often sets a pot, of *menudo*, *pozole*, *cocido* or any other soup, to cook. Long after the tortillas are being sampled by fans like myself, her soup is adding its subtle, good aroma, creating a feast for the senses.

Tortillas are made from the simplest of ingredients: flour, lard, salt and water. The dough is mixed by hand and then is divided into little balls about 2½ inches in diameter. They are patted out flat in a certain method, which is called *tortillar* in Spanish. They then are placed on the hot comal and are cooked lightly. (I do not let my grandchildren do that part).

Cruzita makes very big tortillas, and she does a special maneuver of her own. As you practice, you will refine your style. Size and shape are not important. *Recién hecha* tortillas, right off the comal, are tasty anywhere—even in Germany. In fact, a letter from a Tucsonan on behalf of a friend in Germany prompted this week's recipe:

Dear Alva: Would you be so kind as to send me the recipe for making flour tortillas? It is for a young German who loves Mexican food and is a cook in the German Air Force.
Signed, LVP.

Dear LVP: Here is a basic recipe that yields 16 medium-sized flour tortillas:

## FLOUR TORTILLAS
4 cups of flour
6 tablespoons of lard
2 teaspoons of salt
¼ cup of warm water

1. In a bowl, mix flour, lard and salt, working well with your hands until it is the texture of coarse meal.

2. Add warm water and continue working until it blends into a solid mass. Now it is *masa* (dough).

3. Remove the masa onto a flat surface and knead it for about 5 minutes.

4. Cover the masa with a light coat of lard and allow it to rest for at least 10 minutes. It can be refrigerated at this point overnight.

5. Knead it again for 3 to 4 minutes and then squeeze some masa between your thumb and index finger. The result should be a little ball (*bolita*), 2½ inches in diameter.

6. Cover the bolitas lightly with lard and again allow to rest 10 to 15 minutes.

7. Pick one up and pat it out between the palms of your hands. This is called "tortillar."

8. Press the edges of the tortillas firmly with your fingers. Continue "tortillando" and finally, with either hand, begin to stretch the raw tortilla as it rests on your opposite hand and arm, passing it back and forth. Carefully place it on the hot cooking surface.

9. In a few seconds, flip the tortilla over and then back again to the first side.

# Some Edible Ideas for That First *Picinici*

In the "olden days," as my children say, the first big *picinici* each season was held where Sabino Otero's cattle used to meander. On Memorial Day, families would get together, all generations included, and drive out caravan style to el Canyon de Sabino.

The leader would drive around until he found the perfect spot. He would stop and get out, followed by all the rest of the men parking and getting out of their cars. They would peaceably discuss the area. Finally, a few women would get out and join in the discussion. We children would always stay in the cars. Everyone would get back in the cars again and drive around some more looking for perfection.

This would be repeated several times, while the children were sure night would fall and that we would be still driving around. The women would begin to worry that the food might spoil, but mostly about the children getting restless. Finally, at one of the "conferences" everyone would agree that this at last was the perfect place. Everyone pitched in carrying something to the picnic site, which still entailed a walk.

We rarely had a picnic in the same place twice, but miraculously each time it was perfect. The truth is, you could not find a bad spot if you tried.

This coming memorial weekend, picinici or not, you might like to try a favorite potato salad.

### ENSALADA DIVINA
    2 pounds of potatoes
    ½ large sliced red onion
    12 oz jar of marinated jalapenos with carrots

8 oz jar of Italian dressing

Oregano, salt and pepper to taste

1. Cook, peel and slice the potatoes.
2. Layer all of the ingredients and sprinkle with spices.
3. Add the salad dressing and marinate overnight.
4. Before serving, add jalapeno juice to taste.

# Dia de San Juan Food May Usher in Monsoons

Besides El Dia de San Agustín, the day commemorating Tucson's patron saint, El Dia de San Juan was the next most important *dia de santo* in the Old Pueblo.

By tradition, El Dia de San Juan was anticipated by the citizens of the Old Pueblo as being the day heralding the rainy season, lately called the monsoon season.

In days past, everybody would get together and spend the whole day at the Santa Cruz River, while visiting, eating, telling stories, betting, playing games, washing their hair, and bathing in the river.

Two of the foods that always were included, along with the beans, tortillas and salsa, were *salpicon* (sliced tongue) and watermelons. The watermelons were placed in the river water, to keep them cool. The salpicon was placed on blocks of ice in the shade of the tall trees that dotted the banks of the river. Some people wanted to spend the whole day, so they would be out there by sunup and even cook breakfast outside, thereby saving the salpicon for lunch. Leftovers would make up the evening meal. Some diehards would build bonfires and stay there singing and relaxing until the day was completely over.

Salpicon is basically a cool meat and vegetable platter, traditionally made with tongue. But for those who don't care for tongue, it can be made by using the same recipe, but by substituting sliced, cooked roast beef or slices of cooked chicken or turkey. However, tongue is the original ingredient. The basic recipe follows:

Salpicon
   1 tongue
   1 pound of small potatoes

1 pound of summer squash
1 pound of beets
1 pound of sweet potatoes
1 cup of the marinade, made of vinegar, oil, and herbs

1. Simmer tongue in water until tender, for about 3 hours.
2. Cool, peel, and slice.
3. Parboil the vegetables.
4. Arrange alternate slices of tongue and vegetables on platter.
5. Drizzle on the marinade, cover and refrigerate.
6. At serving time, garnish with egg slices.

In another version, instead of slicing everything, you cut the vegetables in different shapes and add quarters of tomatoes, slices of bell pepper and slices of cucumbers, as well as cut green beans and asparagus. Arrange all of the vegetables, parboiled and uncooked, along with the sliced tongue. Drizzle the prepared marinade over all and sprinkle the dish with salt and pepper to suit.

I like to make a special marinade, which includes jalapeno juice and tiny slices of red onion, along with vinegar, oil, rosemary, oregano and bits of fresh garlic.

All of this is just to give you an idea, and you can include any vegetables your family prefers, of course. I make my marinade a few days ahead of time, so that all the flavors blend well. If you don't have time for that, use any prepared favorite dressing or just plain vinegar and oil. The basic salpicon does not include any chili at all.

I hope it rains Monday. If so, I'll be at the Santa Cruz, at least wetting my hair.

# Take Tourists Downtown for a Change

If you are lucky enough to have summer visitors, instead of taking them to the better-known tourist attractions, such as the Desert Museum or San Xavier Mission, you might consider the downtown area. Include the Tucson Museum of Art, 140 North Main Avenue, now featuring *Native Faces: Indian Cultures in American Art*. Also include the Sosa-Carrillo-Fremont House at 151 South Granada Avenue, and the Garden of Gethsemane near the Congress Street bridge on the banks of the Santa Cruz River.

I remember that as children, we would go to watch Felix Lucero make the religious figures from the Santa Cruz River sand right on the western bank. Every time we got a summer rain, however, the figures would wash away. My father would drive us over the bridge to see if the water had reached the statues yet. Eventually, the statues would dissolve and disappear. The next summer, Señor Lucero would start his labor of love all over again. Lucky for us that he finally made the statues out of a more durable material and located them at a slightly higher elevation on the riverbank.

I also recall the building across the river on the northeast side, called the Riverside Auditorium [645 West Congress Street], and I slightly recall the marathon dances held there. We neighborhood kids always wanted to stay and see who would win, but of course that was

FIGURE 2.4 Advertisement. *Citizen*, December 7, 1940, p.5.

FIGURE 2.5  Felix Lucero Park: Garden of Gethsemane at 670 West Congress Street in 2021. Photo taken by Lydia R. Otero.

impossible. The other day, I saw a dull contest in which people had to continually stand and touch a vehicle, until the last person was left touching the vehicle would win it.

It seemed to me that it was a lot more fun watching those earlier marathon dancers, while hearing the music and watching the colored lights being turned low and then bright—and watching others watching. What I could never figure out was how the musicians stayed awake. I guess some of them took time to sleep and eat. I always wondered about who won.

From there, on the way home we would pass by El Tiradito, also known as the Wishing Shrine to see all the candles. But that's a whole other story. I will only mention that the shrine also is downtown on South Main Avenue, a block south of the Tucson Community Center complex.*

---

*The Tucson Community Center's name was changed to the Tucson Convention Center in 1988.

August 14, 1985

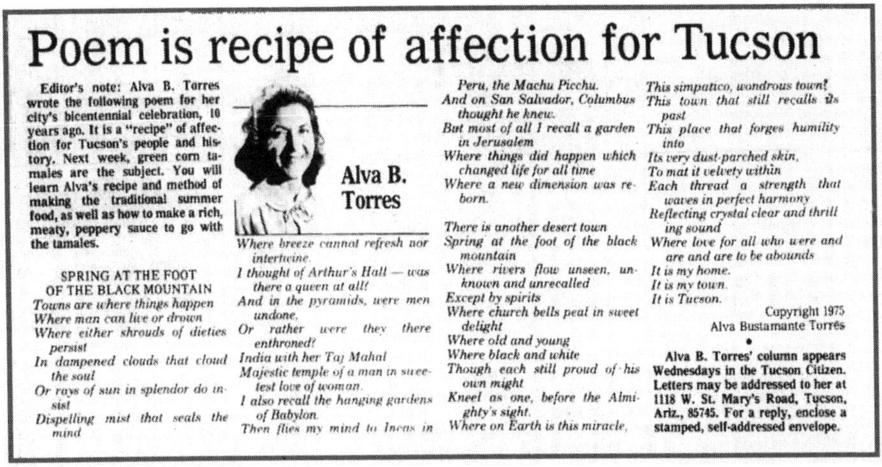

# Poem is Recipe of Affection for Tucson

*Citizen Editor's note: Alva B. Torres wrote the following poem for her city's bicentennial celebration, 10 years ago. It is a "recipe" of affection for Tucson's people and history.*

SPRING AT THE FOOT OF THE BLACK MOUNTAIN
*Towns are where things happen*
*Where man can live or drown*
*Where either shrouds of deities persist*
*In dampened clouds that cloud the soul*
*Or rays of sun in splendor do insist*
*Dispelling mist that seals the mind*
*Where breeze cannot refresh nor intertwine.*
*I thought of Arthur's Hall—was there a queen at all?*

FIGURE 2.6  Column. *Citizen*, August 14, 1985, p. 3B.

*And in the pyramids, were men undone,*
*Or rather were they there enthroned?*
*India with her Taj Mahal*
*Majestic temple of a man in sweetest love of woman.*
*I also recall the hanging gardens of Babylon.*
*Then flies my mind to Incas in*
*Peru, the Machu Picchu.*
*And on San Salvador, Columbus thought he knew.*
*But most of all I recall a garden in Jerusalem*
*Where things did happen which changed life for*
*    all time*
*Where a new dimension was reborn.*

FIGURE 2.7 Mid-1970s photo of Alva B. Torres who was active in the efforts to place markers on principle downtown streets that beckoned back to the city's territorial days. Courtesy Alva B. Torres.

*There is another desert town*
*Spring at the foot of the black mountain*
*Where rivers flow unseen, unknown and unrecalled*
*Except by spirits*
*Where church bells peal in sweet delight*
*Where old and young*
*Where black and white*
*Though each still proud of his own might*
*Kneel as one, before the Almighty's sight.*
*Where on Earth is this miracle,*
*This simpatico, wondrous town?*
*This town that still recalls its past*
*This place that forges humility into*
*Its very dust-parched skin,*
*To mat it velvety within*
*Each thread a strength that waves in perfect harmony*
*Reflecting crystal clear and thrilling sound*
*Where love for all who were and are and are to be abounds*
*It is my home.*
*It is my town.*
*It is Tucson.*

Copyright 1975
Alva Bustamante Torres

# Candles Still Being Lit at El Tiradito Wishing Shrine

This coming Saturday, it will be 14 years since El Tiradito wishing shrine was placed on the National Register of Historic Sites. It is on South Main Avenue, in the block south of the Community Center and directly south of El Minuto Restaurant.

Arnulfo Trejo, Victoria Welch and Rosendo Perez, along with the Tiradito and Placita committees, were instrumental in saving this folklore shrine, which then had been in the way of the [proposed and] since-canceled Butterfield freeway route.

El Tiradito involves several popular legends and goes back well over 100 years. This shrine is strictly folkloric and is not acknowledged by any established religion. Nevertheless, it is popular to this day.

FIGURE 2.8 El Tiradito in the 1920s. Courtesy Special Collections, University of Arizona Library.

FIGURE 2.9  El Tiradito in 2021. Photo taken by Lydia R. Otero.

I recall that during World War II, the melted wax was so thick from the multitude of candles that were being lighted continually, that sometimes the city sent crews to remove the slippery wax, lest someone might slip and fall. During the times of big battles, you could smell the odor of the candles. Here is one of the shrine's legends:

In the 1870s, Dr. F. H. Goodwin owned a ranch some miles north of Tucson. He employed Juan Oliveros, who with his young wife and his father-in-law, lived at the ranch. According to the legend, the doctor accused Juan of being infatuated with his mother-in-law and suspected hanky-panky. One day, when Juan went into the Old Pueblo on a buying trip, his father-in-law followed him. When he saw with his own eyes Juan leave the mother-in-law's house by way of the back door, he was sure he was betrayed. He followed Juan.

As Juan passed by a woodpile, the doctor picked up an ax, which he hurled at Juan in a fury. The ax landed on Juan's back, killing him instantly. Because

Juan died "in sin," his body could not be buried in a sanctified plot, so he was buried where he fell.

Many felt that an innocent man had been murdered, and so they came to light candles at his grave and to pray for his soul, sinner or not. Some of the faithful asked for miracles on his innocent blood. Soon they noticed that when their particular candles continued burning all night, coincidentally their prayers were answered too.

The legend continued to grow and spread throughout the area. The ground became known as El Tiradito, or "The Castaway." English-speaking people called it the Wishing Shrine. Except for rainy nights, candles still are lit there and some burn all night and wishes still come true, they tell me.

# 1986

# *Caldos* Delicious, Simple to Prepare

Some of the best and easiest dishes to cook during this time of the year are are *caldos*, or soups. A popular one is simply called *fideo*, which is vermicelli. Another one is *sopa de maccaron*, or macaroni soup.

FIDEO FOR TWO
1 tablespoon of cooking oil
1 garlic bud
¼ onion
1 vermicelli roll or coil
1 fresh tomato
3 cups of chicken or beef stock
salt and pepper to suit

1. Place the cooking oil and garlic bud in a heavy soup pot or pan and brown the garlic so it is easy to spot.
2. Thinly slice the onion and sauté.
3. Break up the vermicelli and brown it lightly.
4. Quarter the tomato and add it.
5. Finally add the stock and condiments.
6. Bringing it to a high simmer until the vermicelli is done.

Another version of this same recipe, which vegetarians might enjoy, is to precook pinto beans, saving all the liquid and adding that bean liquid in place of the stock. It is equally savory.

Our second recipe today also can be made two ways. It can be made in what we call *sopa seca*, which literally means "dry soup," but is in reality about

the consistency of a stew. Or it can be made *caldoso,* which means soupy.
Here is the recipe for the first:

### SOPA DE MACARRON SECA
1 tablespoon of oil
1 garlic bud
1½ onion, sliced
2 tablespoons of fresh tomato or tomato sauce
1 cup of macaroni
¼ pound of longhorn or jack cheese
½ cup of liquid
salt and pepper to suit

1. Slice the vegetables and sauté all of them in the oil.
2. Add the macaroni and brown it lightly.
3. Now add the liquid, which can be water or stock.
4. Cook until the macaroni is done.
5. Dice the cheese and add it along with the salt and pepper.

In the second version, you add stock and sliced carrots and zucchini. All
of these tastes good with *bolillos,* which are small, individual Italian-style
loaves, available at all Mexican food stores and many of the supermarkets
on the West Side.

# Fond Memories of Tucson Rodeo Days

La Fiesta de los Vaqueros is rodeo time in the Old Pueblo and time for our famous parade.

I urge everyone, especially our welcomed visitors, to be sure to see it live. Nothing can compare to seeing the magnificent horses and hearing the high-spirited school marching bands and being in the midst of the lively crowd.

I think of our landlady, Señora Jesus "Chu" Flores, when I reminisce about rodeo parades. We moved into the upstairs of her home in 1936, at 35 East McCormick Street, next to the Temple of Music and Art. The parade passed by on the corner of Stone Avenue and McCormick Street. She never missed one and neither did we.

After Señora Flores was widowed she converted the downstairs—which had been the carriage room, the stables and her former husband's office and study into her home. She rented the upstairs, which had been her home, to us. It was an interesting two-story house. Her husband was a builder who built, among other structures, the old St. Augustine and Holy Family Church.

The house was set far back in the lot, fronted by Señora Flores' garden. In it she had many rose bushes, vines and hedges, trees, flowers, two wood-slat benches, stones and big bird cages. One of them housed a nightingale that warbled the sweetest trill.

An even larger cage was in her converted carriage room, which served as a multipurposed living-dining-card-siesta room, weather permitting. The former stables became her kitchen and her husband's study and office became her bedroom. In her bedroom, in the wooden floor beneath the rug, was a secret door. It led down some stairs into a wine cellar. This is where, during Prohibition, the holy wine was kept. She said it was not holy yet, but after it

FIGURE 3.1 A side view of Alva's childhood home undergoing renovations in 2021. A portion of the Temple of Music and Art is on the left. Photo taken by Lydia R. Otero.

was slipped out through a little window on the west wall of the former stables to the priests, it was holy.

It all sounded mysterious and intriguing, especially to a child brought up in the Mexican Methodist church. Next to the converted carriage room was a tiny yard with a single small fig tree and a shed. Here Señora Flores toasted aromatic coffee beans and that wonderful aroma would rise upstairs and often waft us into a gentle wakefulness. Anything she cooked had a good aroma.

Speaking of good and appetizing aromas, let us get to our recipe. Today we are eating a dish locally called *posole* or *pozole*. According to one of the Islas

FIGURE 3.2  Temple of Music and Art on 330 South Scott Avenue. Photo taken in 2021 by Lydia R. Otero.

brothers,* what we in Tucson call pozole is called *gallina tina* in some parts of Mexico. This is very curious because *gallina*, which means chicken, is not an ingredient in either one. Instead both of them are cooked with all or any of the following meats: *Chamorros*, shank or soup rings: *puerco*, pork and *cola*, tail. The only thing certain is that we always include *nixtamal*, raw maize.

The recipe is very simple, and remember: this is just a guideline and you can vary the different ingredients to suit your palate. It does freeze well. With a simple tossed salad or coleslaw, *bolillos*, and a light dessert you have a meal worthy of even a *vaquero*.

### TUCSON POZOLE

2 pounds of one or a combination of soup rings, pork neck bones, and/or ox tail

1 pound of nixtamal (hominy)

---

*The Islas brothers owned and operated the American Meat Co. located at 1439 South Fourth Ave. Their business closed in 2015.

1 pound of pinto beans
1–2 whole red chiles
½ an onion
1 small whole head of garlic
½ bunch of cilantro, divided
2 quarts of water
Salt to taste

1. In a 2½ quart capacity soup pot, place everything except the salt. Mix it up so that all the ingredients are dispersed.

2. Bring it all to a boil and then lower the heat to a mild to medium simmer. Cook until the beans are done and the nixtamal begins to "flower," then add the salt and cook just a few minutes longer.

3. Garnish with the second half of the cilantro, which you should chop into small pieces. Some people like to use chopped green onion: others prefer salsa or oregano sprinkled on top.

# Victory Garden Tasty but Not Quite Winner

When planting time comes around, I fondly recall the best garden we ever planted. It was during World War Il. Everyone was supposed to help the war effort by planting a Victory garden.

Senora Jesus "Chu" Flores, our landlady, gave us a small plot of ground in her garden. It was near the front hedge by our favorite playhouse—the chinaberry tree. We begged her to let us have it, telling her we wanted to help the war effort. After all our *tío* Mario, *tío* Hector, *primo* Rick and neighborhood friend Alberto were all serving our country overseas.

We decided not to plant beans. Mother and Father brought these from Mexico, so we did not think it would help much to grow them. We ended up with radishes, lettuce and carrots. We had rows of them and we followed their progress and helped them along.

One day, we decided the soil looked too dry, so we watered the plants two ways. One way was under the watchful eyes of Señora Flores. Poor Señora Flores. The rent for our home was only $20 a month and that included the water for family of five. So the other way we watered—every chance we got, night and day—was by carrying half gallon glass milk bottles from upstairs, down to the vegetables, without her watchful eyes.

We could not wait to harvest our crops and I guess neither could the animals because they began to eat up everything almost as fast as it was visible. Leaves and all. We were dismayed, and so rather than lose it all, we harvested early. These were the tastiest three-inch carrots I ever ate. And they were the last Victory garden vegetables we ever planted, too.

The water bill must have jumped up because Señor Flores convinced us it would be much better to let her plant her usual flowers. She said we could help the war effort more effectively by taking flowers to the church altar. She was sure that the *Virgen Maria* and *Tata Dios* would hear our prayers and end the war.

Whatever it was, we always knew we helped our servicemen and the war effort because all of them came home alive and we won the war.

# 'Mother of Bilingual Education' Honored

Tucsonan Maria Urquides is the mother of bilingual education here. She is a dedicated, respected and greatly loved teacher whom all of us in the Spanish-speaking community refer to as Maria, *la madre de la educación bilingue.*

Sunday, Club Recuerdo will honor Urquides at a *tardeada*, or afternoon get-together, for her tireless work to bring equal educationai opportunities to all. It is to be held at the Elks Club, 2404 East River Road, from 2 to 6 p.m. and will feature music by Lalo Robles and his orchestra.* The profits will go to her favorite project: the building of a facility through La Frontera to help target potential child abuse. Tickets for this event are available to the general public.

Maria was born December 9, 1908, at home on Convent Street behind St. Augustine Cathedral. For one year she attended Mansfeld Elementary School, later known as Safford Elementary School. The following year, at her mother's insistence, the family moved because of prostitutes in nearby Gay Alley between McCormick and Jackson streets. Maria said she did errands for the girls, who were very nice to her.

She then attended Holliday school (which later became Tucson High School), then Roskruge. She continued her schooling at Safford Junior High, where Spanish-speaking students were sent, and then went on to graduate from Tucson High School. At that point she left Tucson to study at Tempe State Teachers College [now Arizona State University], where she lived in a dormitory. That caused a scandal. Mexican American girls did not live outside of their parents' home in 1926.

---

*After WW II, Eduardo "Lalo" Robles and his orchestra gained recognition for their "big band" sound and played private venues and in ballrooms throughout Arizona.

FIGURE 3.3  Maria Urquides.
Lydia R. Otero Collection.

Her first teaching assignment was at Davis Elementary School, in one of the poorest districts of Tucson. It was later, when she taught at Sam Hughes Elementary School (1941 to 1948), that she began to see the enormous social contrast in the system. She became concerned about her former students at Davis, where the children were mostly Spanish-speaking and Yaqui (Yoeme), along with a smattering of Asians and blacks. The students were for the most part from low-income families.

At Sam Hughes most of the children were the offspring of lawyers, doctors and University of Arizona faculty members as well as other professionals. The two groups were receiving entirely different kinds of educations. Even the appearance of the schools was different. Maria began to question, "Why couldn't these children be brought together as part of the whole system?"

In 1955 she was sent to Pueblo High School. During her tenure she became totally involved with her students. She said, "I saw the Spanish-speaking students prostituting their names to accommodate the rest of the community, not knowing one damn thing about their culture, not speaking either English or Spanish correctly and having no pride in themselves."

Next week I will try to tell you what she did to help these students.

# Urquides Saw Need for Bilingual Teaching

Maria Urquides continued, on differences she saw between Davis and Sam Hughes schools by saying:

> The attitude of the students at Davis and at Sam Hughes was so different and the fact that the same differences were still evident among the Anglo-American and the Mexican American in high school, awakened me to the fact that we had to change the methodology of teaching so that these latter students would be proud of themselves and be able to achieve success in their studies. They had to be proud of who they were, their culture and their language.
>
> The administrators at Pueblo High School, Elbert Brooks and Florence Reynolds were aware of the students' attitudes also. It was here where we started for the first time a concentrated effort of teaching Spanish to the Spanish speaking. They soon began to identify themselves and become proud of themselves. We could see it made a real difference. It was not just important but vital that the students learn Spanish, because it gave them roots on which to build. We decided that high school was a bit late and that bilingual education should begin at the beginning.

At that time Señorita Urquides was the state representative on the board of the National Educational Association. She went before this board to try to get a grant to go forward with this methodology. The board itself could not fund it, but they encouraged her. She then went to the U.S. Rural Department of Education and they budgeted $2,000. She then talked to school officials here who gave her permission to take fellow educators, Adalberto Guerrero, Rosita Cota and Henry "Hank" Oyama on a tour to the predominately Spanish speaking areas in Colorado, New Mexico, Texas and California, as well as other parts of Arizona. They were to find out how the Mexican American students were doing.

They visited 38 schools and many, many classes. They authored and edited a booklet called, *The Invisible Minority*. It became a NEA publication.*

Guerrero spoke before Congress on behalf of minority students. His efforts and those of the others gave bilingual education its start in this country. Many other men and women were involved, but it was Maria Urquides who spearheaded and pioneered it after having gone through the school system, becoming a teacher and teaching in it. She richly deserves the title "Mother of Bilingual Education."

Despite a harried schedule, Maria always has taken time out for community projects. Among them are the Pio Decimo Center and La Frontera Center Inc. La Frontera currently is at the forefront, and Maria is hoping that money can be raised to build a facility where parents or parents-to-be with mental, alcohol or drug problems can be counseled to avoid abuse of children.† Such children, if parents don't receive counseling, are likely to show up at La Casa de Los Niños, a center for abused or neglected children.

Maria's ardent wish is that such abuse be prevented by working with the parents or people involved with these children. "The site is already prepared. All we need is the funds to build the facility," Maria said. Those wanting to help Maria Urquides in her latest effort may contact La Frontera.

---

*National Education Association of the United States, *The Invisible Minority: Report of the NEA-Tucson Survey on the Teaching of Spanish to the Spanish-speaking* (Washington, D.C.: Dept. of Rural Education, National Education Association, 1973).

†La Frontera Center broke ground for a new Child/Family Center in April 1986 at 502 West 29th Street. As board president, Maria Urquides led the fundraising campaigns and oversaw the construction of the new facility.

# Music and Food Play Cinco de Mayo Roles

Many people know that Cinco de Mayo is some kind of "freedom day" in Mexican history. It is not the day of independence, but it is an important date because it marks the date the Mexicans won a battle against the French in the town of Puebla in 1862.

Celebrations are now in evidence all over Tucson, but in years past the main fiestas or celebrations took place in *ambos* Nogales, mainly in the one south of the border.

During the day, there was a colorful parade that would go through the international border from Nogales, Sonora to Nogales, Arizona, and then back to Sonora again, in which *la reina y su corte*, the queen and her court, were of primary importance.

At night, music was the main event and people attended either a private party, a public dance in a hall or the *perradas* (crowded parties). Those were held along a specified street in Nogales, Sonora adjacent to the railroad tracks. Many individual musical groups from Nogales and as far away as Sinaloa would station themselves every 300 feet for several blocks, ready to entertain the patriots.

People would stroll down the street, enjoying the groups. From across the street, waiters would run over to the audience and take orders for *taquitos, burritos, frijolitos, cerveza*, sodas and more. For an extra tip, they would do anything to be helpful, like bring you cigarettes or a blanket. Many people would dance and sing along with the professional musicians. Others just might listen. But most would have a good time.

The fiesta activities would continue for several nights, continuing until the wee hours. Most Spanish-speaking *Tucsonenses* would be sure to make it for at least one of the celebrations during the several days. Somehow, all Mexican fiestas take more than one day, as you will notice next week as Tucson celebrates Cinco de Mayo.

Speaking of music, another good two-day fiesta is coming up May 9 and 10—the Tucson International Mariachi Conference. It combines a workshop and concerts that are open to the public. This year Linda Ronstadt is the special guest. The second night is Garibaldi night, when the mariachi groups perform outside at the Community Center and various non-profit groups sell food.

Today's recipe is one you find at all the fiestas in our area. I call them *puesto* tacos because these are the ones you will find in the puestos, or booths, as the ingredients can be handled safely in large quantities. We shall make them in a small quantity for a regular meal.

### PUESTO TACOS
1 pound of lean ground meat
1 onion, minced
2 carrots, shredded
2 Anaheim chiles, finely sliced
1 large fresh tomato, diced
1 clove garlic, minced
a pinch of oregano
12 corn tortillas
3 cups finely shredded lettuce and cabbage
½ pound shredded cheese or grated Parmesan
Salsa

1. Brown meat, and the onion, carrots, chiles, tomato, garlic and oregano and cook until tender.

2. Place some filling into center of tortilla: fold in half and secure with a toothpick or two.

3. Repeat with remaining tortillas.

4. Place prepared tortillas into a lightly oiled pan and fry them lightly on both sides; remove to your serving plate.

5. Remove toothpicks and top each taco with lettuce and cabbage mixture.

6. Add grated cheese or Parmesan cheese for ease and an equally good taste.

7. Serve with salsa

I use a very simple salsa made with canned tomato sauce, diluted with water. I add garlic salt, oregano and a dash of lemon or vinegar to it. You can also use prefried taco shells, but they will not taste the same. This along with some beans and a beverage, makes a nice meal with a papaya or mango for dessert. Now, if you can get someone to come over to play the guitar and sing, you can have your own fiesta.

FIGURE 3.4 Advertisement. *Arizona Daily Star*, April 27, 1986, p. 8D.

# Magic Will Continue in ATC's Temple

With a lot of other *Tucsonenses*, I sigh with relief, knowing the Temple of Music and Art, which we called *El Templo de Musica*, will be the future home of the Arizona Theatre Company. It will become a public facility sometime this summer, according to our able City Manager Joel D. Valdez.

As children, my sisters Julietita and Esthersita and I spent a good deal of our playtime inside and outside this building. All three of us thoroughly enjoyed "our castle." I remember coming down the wide staircase as an "unjustly sentenced victim," namely Joan of Arc, more than once. Julietita was at various times a bride or a queen of an imaginary country. Esthersita also had her fantasy trips there, years after her *hermanitas*, sisters, had stopped pretending.

Besides pretend times, we had our real times. Mrs. Healy, the manager, gave the janitor permission to allow us to enter the temple, free of charge, to see the entertainment presented there. Before a show the janitor would tell us, "Get into your Sunday best tonight and come to the front door as soon as all the other people go in. Now don't yuh forget." We would be there for sure and for sure he would open the door and we would go in quietly. Then we would follow him and he would point out empty seats to us.

Between 1938 and 1946, we saw a good many wonderful programs. Among them was Robert Young in "The Enchanted Cottage." One of my highlights was seeing and hearing Tito Guizar [Mexican singer and actor] present a program and sing "Guadalajara." For that show Mrs. Healy had the side exit doors opened wide so all the barrio kids could enjoy it. Only once were we asked to leave because some patrons reported us as sitting in their absent friends' seats. We also saw the first act of "Swan Lake." It was so beautiful.

FIGURE 3.5 All three Bustamante sisters in 1946. Alva in the middle, Julieta on left, and Esther on the right. The photograph was taken at La Nopalera Studios. Courtesy Alva B. Torres.

Later we danced ballet ourselves when we took dancing lessons from Miss Schwabs at the temple.

In our make-believe world, we could never envision our fairyland castle gone. We dreamed it would always be there. So, I say, dreams do come true, not just for us, but for countless people who have enjoyed the Temple of Music and Art, and those who have been interested in saving it over the years. We can still, because of these knights in shining armor, continue to enjoy our *castillo*.

# Ballads, Photos Tell History of Mexico

You are cordially invited to attend an afternoon of *corridos*, or ballads, from the Mexican Revolution. This musical presentation is planned for 2 p.m. Sunday at the Tucson Museum of Art at 140 North Main Avenue.

It is being held in conjunction with the museum's exhibition of *The World of Agustin Victor Casasola: Mexico, 1900–1938*. Although you may not be familiar with his name, you have probably seen some of his photographs. Thirty-five years old at the time of the revolution in 1910, Casasola was at the height of his career as a photojournalist. For the next 28 years he recorded all the events and people that he felt would tell the world about Mexico and its history. In images that speak louder than my words ever could do, he captured the essence and soul of the Mexican Revolution through its people. His photographs of Emiliano Zapata and Francisco "Pancho" Villa made their faces familiar to most of Mexico and the southwestern United States. This exhibition includes more than 150 of his stirring photographs.

The opportunity to view this exhibition, along with the many interesting events, concerts, lectures and films scheduled to take place during the showing, is made available at no charge to the general public. The exhibition demonstrates the importance of liberty and freedom and the unquenchable yearning to be free that lives throughout the ages in the souls of all men. I consider the entire program a salute to liberty. Which is so precious to all of us.

Sunday's focus is on corridos, which are used to describe events or people in music and poetry. Corridos are very popular with the common people. At the time of President John F. Kennedy's assassination, countless corridos were written. A good number were preserved on 45-rpm records by Mexican people and others, lamenting this tragedy that to them was both national and personal. Kennedy was greatly admired and loved by the Mexican people.

Antonio Federico, native of Sasabe, Sonora, born in 1934, will lead the corridos. He sings at Mass and events that mark joyous as well sorrowful times in families' lives. He has been a featured performer at Tucson Meet Yourself and was their prize winner in last year's Corrido competition.

Next Tuesday, the Tucson Museum of Art will present *Los Muertos Nunca Mueren* (The Dead Never Die) by The Borderlands Theater, *Teatro Fronterizo*. The program will feature Francisco Gonzalez from Santa Barbara, California. He has received numerous awards, including the San Francisco Chronicle's "Bernie Award" in 1982, and the Bay Area Theater Critics' Circle Award "for outstanding achievement in the theater in 1983." He regularly performs Jarocho and Norteño music at clubs, fiestas and other social gatherings and has made recordings playing the Mexican harp.

The Tucson Public Library is also offering a series of four public programs in August exploring the events, ideas and people of the Mexican Revolution, 1910–1917, called *Imagenes de la Revolución Mexicana*. Here is the schedule:

- A staged reading of *Las Muertos Nunca Mueren* on August 1 at El Rio Neighborhood Center, 1390 West Speedway Boulevard.
- *Mujeres de la Revolución* (Women of the Revolution) on August 18 at the Valencia Library, 202 West Valencia Road.
- *Corridos de la Revolución Mexicana* (Ballads of the Mexican Revolution) on August 22 at El Pueblo Neighborhood Center, 101 West Irvington Road.
- *La Leyenda de Pancho Villa* (The Legend of Pancho Villa) on August 26 at the Mission Library, 3770 South Mission Road.

The programs begin at 7 p.m.

# The Quinceañera has Become a Fiesta Event

In 1971, 21 young women were presented as Florecitas de Xochimilco by the League of Mexican American Women at their fourth annual Fiesta. They were presented in a modified version of the traditional Mexican quinceañera "coming out," or debut of a 15-year-old girl to society.

Quinceañeras are quite elaborate and have continued in Tucson over the years, becoming more sophisticated as time goes by. They have also become more expensive. The girl to be presented is traditionally dressed in a beautiful white gown, reminiscent of the Southern belle tradition. She is accompanied by 14 other girls dressed in complimentary gowns, all in the same style and all of one color. All of the girls are escorted by male counterparts dressed in tuxedoes. They usually wear accessories that match the gowns. Nowadays it is not unusual to see the entire party brought in limousines to the quinceañera. Also, of late, instead of the families preparing the food for the guests, it might be catered.

An important part of the quinceañera is the Mass, which is the first part of the celebration. It normally is held on the same day as the presentation. In the case of the League's event, it is a celebrated Mass, with Bishop Moreno and Bishop Green, and it is held on the Sunday preceding the event, at St. Augustine Cathedral on South Stone Avenue.

Technically, a girl did not date before her quinceañera. In the "old days," many young women married quite young, often within two years of their presentation, and often to older men who could carry the responsibility of supporting a household. Fifteen might seem like a young age to be presented, but by that time girls had been taught the skills needed to take care of a home and family—cooking, cleaning, darning, sewing, ironing, and other useful things, among them catching a chicken, cleaning it and cooking it. Of

course, tradition dictated that young
women be chaperoned in those days
until the wedding ceremony. Even in
my lifetime there were girls who were
not left alone with their fiancées before
the marriage.

When the League decided to incor-
porate the quinceañera into its Fiesta
de Xochimilco, the members hoped
it would complement the Fiesta and
strengthen cultural ties. It has grown
to be the focal point of the Fiesta. The
money individual parents would have
spent on a private presentation is being
better spent on scholarships and educational funds for the community.

The League of Mexican American
Women has earned itself a good reputation in raising funds and in cultural
endeavors in the community since

FIGURE 3.6 Fiesta en Xochimilco in 1971.
Courtesy Special Collections, University of
Arizona Library.

1967. In 1968, Fresia Terrazas Limberg was elected the League's first president.
This year's president is Gloria Rodriguez, who is already making plans for the
upcoming 20th year anniversary celebration.

Among the recipients of funds have been the Pio Decimo Center and
the YWCA Latchkey program. They have also recognized and honored outstanding women of the community, and in 1975 held the first Arizona conference for Spanish-speaking women. This conference was entitled "*Llego el
Mañana Para la Mujer*," a loose translation is "Tomorrow Has Arrived for
Women." The League members also participate in La Fiesta de la Placita and
the tour of the Kino missions, as well as the Arizona-Sonora Desert Museum,
La Fiesta de los Vaqueros and other worthwhile activities.

On Saturday, September 6, the League will hold its annual Fiesta de Xochimilco at the Tucson Community Center. The public is welcome to attend.
For more information, call Natalia Benites at 325-XXXX or Dee Muñoz at
745-XXXX.

# El Casino Ballroom had a Loyal Following

In spite of the heat and humidity, loyal fans of El Casino Ballroom [437 East 26th Street] turned out by the hundreds on the afternoon of August 10 to celebrate the autobiographical publication of one of its former owners.

Just as the Blue Moon Dance Hall on Miracle Mile is well known to those Tucsonans born prior to the '30s, El Casino Ballroom was the stomping ground for those of us born thereafter. We were there to congratulate and celebrate with Adolfo C. Loustaunau on the publication of his book, *Los Dos Mundos de Fitín*—Fitín being his childhood nickname.* His *dos mundos*— two worlds—deals with his life from his birth, in Urique, Chihuahua, in 1910, through adolescence. His second world, was from the time he arrived in Tucson in the '20s through his adult life. His book includes many photographs and passages on his family, the different places he lived, and various groups of people including the crowd at El Casino Ballroom. His final chapter is his family genealogy and some blank forms to fill your own.

He lived in Hermosillo before coming to Tucson in the late 1920s. Shortly after his arrival here, Loustaunau went to work for Moses Drachman and later for Oliver Drachman, at their laundry. He spoke in Spanish to Loustaunau, asking Loustaunau to reply in English to help him learn the language.

Loustaunau, contractor Ramón V. Siquerios and Benjamín "Benny" Jacobs became business partners and literally built El Casino from the ground up. Electrician Mike Monares helped them. Even the street had to be worked on before they could begin. (At the Casino during the celebration, Loustaunau introduced Drachman as a good friend and as the first customer El Casino

---

*Adolfo C. Loustaunau, *Los Dos Mundos de Fetín: Relato, Auto-biografico* (Hermosillo: A.C. Loustaunau, 1986). This book is available at the Arizona Historical Society and at the Pima County Library.

FIGURE 3.7 *Reynas* at El Casino Ballroom Mexican Independence Day Celebration in 1964. Courtesy Special Collections, University of Arizona Library.

had when the doors opened September 14, 1947.) Once the ballroom opened, it was a success. It boasted an excellent dance floor, large seating capacity and fine musicians. The combination attracted a loyal following of people who loved to dance. Among the well-known bands that played there were the *orquestas* such as the Quinteros, Rob Elías, Nuñes, Lalo Robles, Uchi Hernandez and Louis Leon.

One of the main reasons Loustaunau and his partners decided to build the ballroom was to give the Mexican American community a place to celebrate all kinds of occasions, particularly *La Fiestas Patrias*. This was the top fiesta of the year and the highlight of it was the presentation of *la reyna y su corte*, the queen and her court. Each year, the reyna looked regal in her red velvet cape, full length gown and glittering crown, led around the dance floor on the arm of a young escort in his tuxedo. The tuxedos were either bought or borrowed, since tuxedo rental was unheard of then.

Loustaunau also recounts a 4th of July spent in New York, but the bulk of the book is in great detail about life in the Old Pueblo. The book is written *en español*, and copies are on sale at Flores National Drug Store on South 12th Avenue and American Meat Market on South Fourth Avenue.

# Irma Moreno is the Family Dancer

Irma Moreno is not a professional dancer, but as in many Mexican American families, she is *la bailarina de la familia*, the dancer in the family. She performs traditional Mexican dances, such as the Jarabe Tapatio, the Mexican Hat Dance, at private parties and family reunions around town, and has performed at the Tucson Community Center several times.

I asked Irma when she learned to dance. "I was moving to music before I could walk," she said. "That is what I have been told. Anytime I heard music I would sway and move my feet." She began performing outside the family circle when she was in the first grade at Ochoa Elementary School. "I would perform for school functions," she said. Later she performed at Tucson High School, Salpointe Catholic and Pueblo.

She began taking formal dancing lessons at Pima Community College from instructor Angel Hernandez about 10 years ago. "He (Hernandez) is one terrific teacher, strict, but you learn," Moreno said. She also performs for her students at Los Niños Elementary School. "They love it. I have danced for the whole student body and they stop me in the hall and ask me, 'Are you the tap dancer?' They really enjoy a teacher doing these things. Then they can see us in a different light, having fun, and that, too, is rewarding."

FIGURE 3.8 Irma Moreno in a China Poblana dress in 1986. Courtesy of Irma Moreno.

Moreno says she feels younger when she dances. "Anytime I hear music, I need to move to it. Not only do I enjoy the music rhythm and movement, but I enjoy my audience responding to my happiness in dancing. There is tremendous joy in seeing a smiling audience. I am almost 50 and I am still able to move and make my body do what I want it to do, flexible. I don't feel 50."

She doesn't have a favorite dance. "My favorite dance is the one I am doing at that moment. I make up my own sometimes, I hear the music and I move, I improvise," she said. Is dance her life? "It's like a strong primal urge. My mom, my aunts, are all very talented, they have music in their blood. I can't help it, when I hear music, I have to dance. It's *la herencia*."

# La Placita is Both the Past and the Present

*The return of La Placita. Throughout most of Tucson's history the slice of land now numbered 120 W. Broadway, was known as La Placita. Historically the area has always been Tucson's financial and cultural center. We are pleased to return to part of our past, as we change our name from United Bank Plaza, to La Placita.*

This paragraph was printed on the flap of the invitations to a recent event that has a significance to a good number of native Tucsonans—10,000 at least.

Newcomers have probably never even heard of La Placita. Its original name is La Plaza de la Mesilla and dates back to the early days when Tucson was still part of the Republic of Mexico. At that time Mesilla, in New Mexico, was equivalent to the county seat of Doña Ana County, to which the Old Pueblo belonged.

The Placita is downtown, located across the street from the little triangle park named Veinte de Agosto, where Francisco "Pancho" Villa's statue sits. The street leading into the Plaza from the west was called Calle de la Mesilla. Legend has it that in 1854, after the Gadsden Treaty was signed in Mesilla, New Mexico, whereby Tucson became part of the United States of America, legal papers and documents were burned in the area of the juncture where the Calle enters the Plaza by some Mexican citizens who felt they had been sold out. On the other hand, many citizens were jubilant at the prospect of coming under the protection of the United States.

By 1868 the new cathedral was begun on the East side of the Placita. It was named San Agustín, the same as the first church built inside the Presidio, after Tucson's Patron Saint. Because the area served as the church plaza, people congregated there in a peaceful manner. (The church eventually fell into disrepair and was demolished in 1936.)

*  *  *

In my lifetime, many, many fiestas were held in La Placita. The best known and the last fiestas prior to urban renewal was La Fiesta de La Placita, which was sponsored by the Tucson Festival Society. My own Club Mavis members, our mothers and our boyfriends decorated a booth every year, hoping to win a grand prize. We finally made it one year. And all of us remember the Club Camelia for selling the best *biscochuelos* (cookies) this side of Hermosillo, Sonora.

Under urban renewal, all this was slated to be lost. By 1966, I organized a group of people for the purpose of saving La Placita and its surrounding buildings. At that time El Charro Restaurant was the main Mexican restaurant located in downtown Tucson. The building itself was most interesting and still had the stables in the back. Ronquillo's Bakery, a fine and growing

FIGURE 3.9  La Placita Committee meeting in 1967 or 1968. From left: Grace Esperon, Viola Terrazas, Carmela Bustamante (Alva's mother), Miguel Bustamante (Alva's father), Julieta Portillo and her husband, Ernesto Portillo, Sr.

business, was in the Placita, as was the Rosquist Gallery, Zepeda's Shoe Shop, The Belmont Hotel, The Half Moon Chinese Restaurant and some others, including a barber shop.

We were known as The Society for the Preservation of La Plaza de la Mesilla. Another group headed by Dorothy Haas, known as San Augustine Committee was also interested in saving the area. Although our goals were the same, we had different ideas about the way to go about it. In the end, we helped each other.

Eighteen people were in the initial group, including Alene Smith, Viola Terrazas, Grace Esperon, Ann Montaño and myself. From outside the organization, other women who gave us tremendous help were Sybil Ellingwood, Natalia Leeney and Ann-Eve Johnson.

Within a few months we were able to collect over 10,000 signatures on our petition for saving La Placita. My main recollection is that of Alene Smith typing all the time, and me talking to groups and individuals, explaining what was on the petitions. Esther, my then-little daughter, says that all she can remember of that summer is us sitting outside of Penny's and Jacome's downtown, hour after hour, day after day, week after week in the heat.

Although the old Plaza Theater and the many other places are now just a memory in our hearts, the old El Charro Restaurant walls still stand, with its ancient stables behind. *Gracias a Dios*, the *kiosko* [gazebo or bandstand], the heart of the Placita, survived. Also gracias to La Placita Committee and friends, who cared enough to give their time and energy and money to save La Placita, including a very busy mother of 10, our prayer chairwoman Lorraine Brichta Aguilar and her multitude of *viejitas* (older women), as well as others who prayed for our success.

Because of all of you who helped, we now have a Placita. Here any one can sit and feel the ultimate freedom of a breeze and hear the cathedral bells and recall a culture and heritage we still cherish and remember.

Not only that, we can plan future fiestas *en* La Placita.

# Maria Luisa Tena's *Nacimiento*

Since Maria Luisa Tena arrived in Tucson from Guadalajara in 1968, she has been involved in volunteer work with several groups.

Among these have been Una Noche Plateada, AMOR (a nonprofit group that helps children with birth defects), the Tucson Festival Society, the Bicentennial Committee, the Tucsonenses, the Padrinos at the Tucson Museum of Art and St. Elizabeth of Hungary Clinic Axillary. Most of her contributions involve children and art, in one way or another.

I first worked with her when she served as decoration chairman for the annual fund raiser, the Una Noche Plateada Ball in 1970. We needed someone who could transform the Exhibition Hall into a silvery night—not an easy task. She did a wonderful job of it. Most of her time was then being taken up with helping AMOR. Later, the Tucsonenses assigned her to organize a *posada* for over 200 barrio children at the Saint Augustine Cathedral. She did it beautifully, and with little help, saw to it that each child received a handmade, flower decorated basket filled with candy and nuts.

But when I think of Maria Luisa, it is the *nacimiento*, the nativity, which comes to my mind. In 1978, she belonged to the Padrinos of La Casa Cordova, which is the Mexican Museum belonging to the Tucson Museum of Art. She told Gilbert Aranetta, president of the group, that she would like to make a nacimiento at the Casa Cordova, in memory of her mother, who had recently died.

Her mother was born in Salamanco, Guanajuato, where the nacimiento has a very strong tradition. She said, "Since I remember, I see the nativity scene. At first it was little, when we were little. As we grew older, my mother made it bigger and bigger. Later on, she always won one of the first prizes. Because in Guadalajara, they make it a contest. Every year, [about] three or

FIGURE 3.10  A section of the *nacimiento* crafted by Maria Luisa Leon Teña in 2018. Photo taken by Lydia R. Otero.

four months before Christmas, we went on little trips to the hills and canyons near Guadalajara to pick up all the little trees, *magay, heno y musco*, which we needed for our nacimiento."

"Here," she said, "finding natural plants and keeping them watered became a problem, so she uses plastic plants these days." The first figures were bought on the back street of Nogales, Sonora. They all needed to be repaired or painted, but they carried bargain prices. She did not think twice about it. She bought them, took them home and added noses, ears, wings, painted eyes, crowns, gowns, whatever needed to be done.

In later years, she went to Guadalajara and brought figures which she had specially made—figures she still lends for the nacimiento. Several of those who volunteered to help her have continued to do so for a few years, including Hector and Alicia Laos. Hector eventually built a set of steps on which the nacimiento sits. It takes up most of one room at La Casa Cordova. Maria Luisa donates months of her time and energy to preparing the nacimiento—no easy task, particularly since she fell a few years ago. This year she says her health is better and she has decided to try again.

The first year she included the nativity itself, the annunciation, the three wise men and King David in his castle. Since then she has added scenes of the holy family, the good Samaritan, John the Baptist, Saint Ann with her child in a *ranchito*. Maria Luisa explained that:

Since my mother, we always made a little ranch . . . because Jesus was born in a humble place. This is a bit of folklore from Mexico, so I decided to include it. The new addition this year is little Jesus, when he was lost and found in the temple with the teachers, and was teaching them. Children are the most observant. Some have been coming for several years, and I hear them say, 'Look Mama, this is new, this wasn't here last year.' I love it. I love to see the children enjoy it.

The blessing of the nacimiento by Bishop Manuel D. Moreno this Sunday will mark the official opening for the display. The museum is located at 140 North Main Avenue.

# New Year's is Time for *Buñuelos* Resolutions

It wouldn't be the same if on the New Year I didn't go to El Charro to pick up a calendar, eat some homemade *buñuelos* and make some New Year's resolutions.

For many years, when my children were children, we began the New Year by going to Candelaria Lopez' home in the area fondly called El Hoyo, where we would be treated to buñuelos. (These are like fried tortillas with syrup poured over them, but are not to be confused with either the Indian fry bread or New Mexico sopapillas, in which you cut a pocket and pour the honey inside and out. All three of them are different.)

The last thing I need to do is to make my resolutions. One of the first has to be not to write my columns so close to deadline. Another has to be to stop eating so much good food. And I must force myself to keep my checkbook balanced. I guess we all have the same kinds of resolutions. It's a shame they can't be something like: Take the trip to Spain and Portugal you've always dreamed of taking.

Here's the recipe for buñuelos:

## BUÑUELOS
    2 cups of flour
    ¼ teaspoon of salt
    1 egg
    1 cup of water
    1 teaspoon of sugar
    Shortening for frying

1. Knead masa (dough) as though you were making tortillas or yeast bread.

2. Form the dough into 18 balls.

3. Let sit for 5 or 10 minutes.

4. Roll out like tortillas and deep fry them in hot shortening.

5. Serve with syrup.

## SYRUP

2 cinnamon sticks

3 cloves

3 cups of brown sugar, panocha or half of each

2 to 4 cups of water

1. Boil the cinnamon and cloves in water for about 20 minutes.

2. Add sugar or panocha and simmer.

# 1987

# The Best Mexican Food? In Tucson, of Course . . .

"Tucson: the Mexican Food Capital of the World and Elsewhere!"

Just in case you missed this proclamation during the holiday rush, here is more information. For the last dozen years or so El Charro Restaurant has been advertising itself as "The Mexican Food Capital of the World." Being of a generous nature, however, the owners decided it might be a good idea to share the slogan with all of the city's Mexican restaurants. Mayor Lewis Murphy (who says people from Sonora come to Tucson to get good Sonoran food) and councilman Roy Laos (who has extensive experience with Mexican food) both liked the idea. With the help of the Metropolitan Tucson Convention and Visitors Bureau, they decided to do something about it.

On December 12, a Mexican buffet was scheduled at the Arizona Inn, marked by competitions, speeches and the proclamation. I was one of the speakers. Here's part of what I told the gathering:

By 1910–11, according to our City Directory, we had 16 restaurants and 11 rooming houses. Since then, restaurants have outnumbered almost all other businesses, except for a few years, saloons and now lawyers.

By 1912 we had 24 restaurants, including Mexicano, Sonorense, Star, Togo and Union, which had Mexican proprietors. El Charro and Lerua's are by far the oldest dating back to 1922. Both Pancho's and la Casa Molina go back to 1947.

Today, many advertise themselves as having authentic Mexican food, including Araneta's Mexican Inn, Karichimaka, El Torero, El Payaso, Tia Elena's, La Parilla Suiza and Papagayo. Some, like Arroyo and Las Capanas de las Catalinas, have Spanish names, but do not specialize in Mexican food, and others, like the Double L, Club 21 and Crossroads, do just the reverse.

Not counting Taco Bells and such, we have more than 50 restaurants serving Mexican food.

What makes our food the best? One reason is that there has always been plenty of competition and only the best can survive. As El Charro's Carlotta Flores told me, "We don't mind things that take longer to cook. We still make our chile, our own *carne seca*. We use fresh produce—red and green chile, cilantro, oregano, onions, garlic, *canela, panocha*."

In Tucson if you ask for *albondigas*, you get albondigas. If you ask for *cocido*, you get cocido made from scratch. That is what built Micha's—the *caldos*. You can still get good menudo at such places as Alberto's, El Zarape and La Suprema. You ask for a chimichanga and you get a chimichanga at Gordo's and Don Juan's.

I have to mention those restaurants that stay open to the wee hours of the morning to accommodate *los alboratados*, who have to eat after the fiestas and *bailes*: Mi Nidito, El Dorado and El Minuto are among the best known. We also have our share of "mom-and-pop" places—where the cooks know us by name, or at least by dish—among them, Rosa's, La Indita Cafe and La Hacienda.

New Mexico has good food, but it is not Mexican—it is handed down Spanish cuisine, overpowered by *comino* (cumin). Texas had good food, but it is not Mexican—it is "Tex-Mex," and red chile is their claim to fame. California has good food, but everyone coming from over there wants to take some food back from here. Mexico has good food, but they should taste a burro from El Rapido.

# City had Stage Lines, 28 Hotels in 1912

On February 14, 1912, Arizona became the 48th state. Here is a glance at what Tucson was like back then:

- The city comprised 10 square miles and had a population of 22,500.
- The police force consisted of a police chief, two sergeants and six patrolmen.
- The Fire Department consisted of five firemen and 30 volunteers.
- Dr. Ira E. Hoffman was mayor.
- There were four hospitals in the city.
- The city's directory was printed by the *Citizen*. It listed streets, two of which have disappeared: Hospital Road, which was located between Main and Fifth; and Kings Highway, a continuation of East 22nd Street.
- Another section of the directory informed readers that it cost 1 cent to mail a postcard. Letters to the United States, Canada, Mexico, Panama, Cuba, Germany, Great Britain, Ireland and China costs 2 cents for each ounce. There was a section with charts on weights and measures, and their metric equivalents.
- Another section contained information on antidotes for poison. The first instruction: Call the doctor. The second instruction: Induce vomiting by tickling the throat with a feather or your finger.
- The directory listed the following schools, including their principals and teachers: Davis, Drachman, Holladay, High School, Mansfeld and Safford.
- By that year the directory already had a listing under the heading of "Art."
- You could arrive in Tucson in 1912 by one of three stage lines or one of five railroads, including one from Mexico. After you arrived you could pick up one of six newspapers, including *El Fronterizo*, printed in Spanish. We had two telephone and telegraph companies and businesses had phones.

- If you needed to reach someone at home, the city had five messenger services. One, McGee, had a slogan "Get messenger boys any minute."
- After arriving you could stay at any of our 28 hotels and rooming houses, including one named Aguirre that to this day still has a stone block proclaiming its existence. When you decided to move somewhere there were four transfer companies to help you. If you needed to find a place to live there were 23 real estate companies that could sell you insurance and lend you money as well as help you find a home.
- Tucson had four banks. The town also had four collection services to contend with and 47 lawyers.
- You could call on one of three architects to help design your home. To build it, you could enlist the help of two brick manufacturers and 26 contractors and builders. We also had listed five painters and wallpaper hangers and six plumbers and tinners [early sheet metal fabricators].
- To get you from here to there Tucson had six carriage services.
- There were eight livery stables and 12 businesses listed under "Blacksmiths and Horse Shoes," as well as four "Hay and Grain" establishments. If this was not your mode of transportation, you could try bicycles.
- For the more affluent, there were nine automobile and repair shops. This included Cadillac, Ford and Mitchell cars. To play it safe, one sold harnesses and saddles.

I'll write more about Tucson's past next week.

# Santa Cruz has Colorful History

Many people are familiar with San Xavier, but not as many of you are acquainted with the church at 22nd Street and South Sixth Avenue, Santa Cruz (Holy Cross) Church. Nevertheless, it has been in Tucson since 1919. Staffed by the Carmelites Descalsos since its inception, the church is celebrating its Diamond Jubilee this year.

I have a copy of *El Tucsonense*, a Spanish-language newspaper, dated February 8, 1919. A story in the paper fills us in a bit about the church's history.

The Most Rev. Henry Granjon, Bishop of Tucson, had resolved to found a convent in what was then one of the outlying areas of the city. Planning began in 1916, when the bishop began procuring materials and Papago (Tohono O'odham) Indians began making adobe bricks, at $10 for each 2,000. The bishop drew up a floor plan for the convent that resembled the plan of Spanish convents, especially the one in Ávila.

Construction of the church started on Monday, November 13, 1916, by contractor Manuel G. Flores and under the direction of the bishop. By the time the church was blessed and inaugurated much had been donated by Tucson women. Here is the list of the first offerings:

- Two artistic angels sustaining a shell for holy water, by Senora Doña Amalia de Mimiaga and Senora Doña Maria de Amado.
- One baptismal font (basin), by Senora Doña Sofia de Sutherland.
- Two lamps, Doña Antonia de Brichta.
- Ten candlesticks for the main altar, Doña Catalina de Carrillo.
- Two candlesticks, each held by an angel, Doña Juanita de Elías.
- A magnificent silver ciborium (a canopy that covers an altar) for Communion, Senora Doña Carmela de Lawton.

FIGURE 4.1  Plaque on Santa Cruz Church. Photo taken by Lydia R. Otero.

- Two candelabras, one set by Doña Josefa de Felix and another by Senora Doña Enriqueta Pratt de Johnson.

Also, Senorita Doña Teresa de Amado presented six magnificent chairs and a table for the living room or parlor, and Senora Doña Maria de Amado donated a rug.

# Glittery Memory Still Leaves its Vestiges

When I think of stars, I think of the way they looked in Prescott, when my sister Julietita and I attended summer camp, or else here in Tucson, at El Casino Ballroom. Not too long ago I attended a benefit *tardeada* (afternoon gathering) there to raise funds for medical and funeral expenses incurred by Tony Corral, a singer who dedicated himself to bringing all of his friends a lot of happiness and who sang at El Casino and other dance halls. I noticed a few wooden stars over the lights. I couldn't help but recall the first time I saw *estrellitas*, little stars, above the best and most popular dance floor we ever had in Tucson, after the famous Blue Moon was gone.

The El Casino, as it is called, still has the largest and smoothest dance floor in town. The ballroom at 425 East 26th Street still is a place where entire families attend dances. When it was first built, there was no ceiling over the dance floor, only a slanted, corrugated roof. I was then a member of Club Mavis [1949], one of several social clubs for unmarried women. We were 25 young women, full of enthusiasm and energy, looking for projects and fun. We decided on a formal spring dance to raise funds for needy children. We wanted to hold the dance at El Casino but we didn't care for the ceiling, so we decided that we should make a ceiling of some type.

We finally voted to cover the ceiling with blue crepe paper and to put stars on the paper. So, for months we met, tracing stars out of thin cardboard and cutting them out. We made several thousand of them. After that we brushed each one with glue and doused them with silver glitter. Then we carefully placed them in boxes to transport from meeting to meeting. Later we stapled each star individually to reams of dark blue crepe paper. This took weeks to finish.

The next step was to sew the strips of paper together. For this we used Mrs. [Elvira] Villaseñor's old sewing machine. Then we drafted all of our boyfriends, uncles and cousins and anyone else to nail wooden strips all across the ceiling in both directions to have some extra reinforcement for the new *cielo* [ceiling].

Finally, we had a "party" to help us nail the crepe paper and stars to the beams and new lattice strips. As if that wasn't enough, we added streamers around the edge of the dance floor and cut them out in arches to match the booths where the people sit. I must say it looked heavenly.

It must have looked pretty good to everyone else, too, because the night of the dance, even though all of us were in long formals, the ceiling was the big hit. My mother sewed our dresses, as always. Mine was a blue moray taffeta with seed pearls, in loops at the sweetheart neckline and cap sleeves, with a huge bow, almost like a bustle. Julieta's was full-skirted white tulle with silk flowers. All of the Club Mavis members received corsages, as did our *mamacitas* and chaperones. Mrs. Villaseñor was our guest of honor.

We had as much fun working together on decorating the place as we had at the Stardust dance itself. There have been a multitude of dances since then at El Casino but no one ever went to that much trouble again. Neither Mr. [Augustine] or Mrs. Villaseñor ever mentioned the fact that we burned up her old sewing machine. She always attended our dances with her daughters Beatrice and Elvira until the day they married.

# Cinco de Mayo Reminds of Freedom

*Citizen Editor's Note: Cinco de Mayo takes on a new significance this year. Columnist Alva Torres departs from her usual subject matter of Mexican food and Mexican heritage to comment. Torres is head of the Immigration Counseling Services Legalization Program for Catholic Community Services.*

\* \* \*

It is ironic that the first date to file for amnesty is today, May 5, the same as the date on which Mexicans and Mexico celebrate the victory of the 1862 battle against the French in Puebla. Maybe the day will benefit illegal (undocumented) immigrants who came to live here before Jan. 1. 1982, the Special Agriculture Workers (SAW) and for the rest of us.

The first "battle" to be fought by illegal (undocumented) immigrants in gaining amnesty under the Immigration Reform and Control Act of 1986 is to answer the proposed, 13-page preregistration form. Today is the first day that those who qualify under the act can apply for amnesty. The form takes into consideration immigrants who will be seeking amnesty in one or more of the following categories:

- Legalization;
- As Special Agricultural Worker (SAW):
- For Cuban/Haitian adjustment
- For Registry

Among the questions to be answered are the normal background questions, such as name, and some not so normal, such as other names used. This one can be quite involved because many people have traditionally used both their mother's and father's surnames. It will also involve maiden names. Many of them are long and not easy for computers. Applicants are also asked to provide information concerning parents, brothers and sisters, and ex-spouses, as well as their spouses and children, the latter understandably so. It asks for dates and places of birth, whether the brothers and sisters are U.S. citizens or lawful U.S. residents. It also asks if those relatives are applying for amnesty and if so, are they applying with the applicant.

This is some of the preregistration information necessary to gain 18 months' temporary residency. After the applications are ready, applicants will be fingerprinted, photographed and will have to have a medical exam-ination. If all goes well, they will have won the first "battle." The applicants' determination reminds me of the pioneer spirit and like the pioneers, they will have to meet many challenges. It is not easy to leave one's native land and look for a better life. They come knowing they are assured of nothing.

They often come with little or no understanding of English. But that will change soon, because during their 18 months of temporary residency, they will need to matriculate in an English class and also will have to learn the U.S. Constitution. At the end of the 18 months, they will be tested on their understanding of both before receiving their permanent residency card. If you know someone eligible to apply for amnesty, you can help them by giving them this information so they can begin to assemble it now. And those of you who are willing to help the applicants more can do so by getting them to classes to learn English or to use it more frequently if they already know it. Encourage them to speak it, no matter how much of an accent they might have. I remember years ago someone saying that he could never understand why it was thought so chic to have a French accent yet so degrading to have a Spanish accent. Accents make life more interesting. An accent gives us part of our personality. It adds color to our speech, and sometimes it is pure fun. So, what if "chair" is pronounced "share"? *Feliz* Cinco de Mayo! Start practicing!

# Honoree's Parents Recall Days of Past

The first thing I noticed when I went to visit Edith Auslander's parents was a sign hanging over the door that said "Casa Sayre."

I was visiting the Sayres because Auslander, one of their four children and human resources director for Tucson Newspapers Inc., had been honored earlier this year as Woman of the Year by the Tucson Metropolitan Chamber of Commerce.

Her father, William, or, as his friends know him, Bill, was born in Patagonia in 1914. In 1919 his mother died, and his father moved the family to Tucson. He attended several local schools. I asked him how he felt about attending so many schools and he said, "I didn't seem to mind it. I was active in sports and played on the baseball and football teams. Tucson was very small then, about 20,000 and a very nice town. I knew practically everybody in town by their first name. We never had any luxuries but my dad was very good to us; we were never neglected."

Sayre held several jobs, but his main one was a locomotive engineer position that he held for 40 years. He retired in 1980. For the last five or six years, he has taught a class once a week. "I take over a few kids who don't know English and tutor them until they can get along. Then I take a few more," he said.

Meanwhile, Micha, his wife, sat by quietly. She is from the Castellan family. Micha attended the old Santa Cruz Convent. "The school was very small and we attended in mixed groups, boys and girls. There was never any prejudice there," she said. Micha went on to Tucson High School, where she graduated in 1929. In 1931, she and Bill met, and after a five-year courtship they were married November 7, 1936, at St. Augustine Cathedral.

I asked Micha about her childhood and she recalled, "Father would tell us we had to go to Mass on Sunday morning if we wanted to go with the

MICKEY MOUSE
SPECIAL
CANDY
ICE CREAM CONES
DRINKS - - - LUNCHES

Make this Your Palace for Sweets

PALACE of SWEETS
125 E. CONGRESS

FIGURE 4.2  Advertisement. *Citizen,*
August 27, 1931, p.9.

family on our Sunday outing. We used to take a streetcar to the University of Arizona with our parents and go to the museum or picnic. On the way home, we would stop at Congress Street and Stone Avenue at the Palace of Sweets. Here we met people and ate ice cream and sodas and had a good time. But if you didn't go to Mass, you couldn't go to any of this."

Bill added that he also used to go to the Palace of Sweets. Then they would get back on the streetcar for the ride home. Micha lived in front of El Tiradito or Wishing Shrine. Bill said, "We didn't lock doors, we slept out in the back yard under the fig trees. We didn't have any coolers." Micha added, "We didn't miss them because we didn't know any better. We had fans and ceiling fans. It was a beautiful life then. I just stayed home and raised the children. We are just very lucky."

Before I left their home, Bill got up and took some *carne seca* from the dining room table. He wrapped it and handed it to me. As he did so, he said, "I make carne seca: I have made it since we got married. I make it the old way, but where the flies don't get to it. I just like to do it." It tasted very good, old-fashioned, simple.

# Torres takes sabbatical
Alva Torres, the native Tucsonan who has written a column on Mexican heritage and Mexican cooking each Tuesday for the Tucson Citizen, has taken a sabbatical. Her column will return in the future.

FIGURE 4.3  Announcement. *Citizen,* June 23, 1987, p. 2D.

1988

# Columnist Returns After Busy 'Vacation'

I have missed writing to all of you and some of you have told me you missed my column, so I am glad to begin once more.

To introduce myself to new readers—or to reintroduce myself to old readers—this space is primarily devoted to recipes, events and people as they reflect or focus on Hispanic life in Tucson, southern Arizona and northern Mexico. If there is a particular recipe which you need or one which you would like to share, let me know.

The reason for my "vacation" was that I was extremely busy directing the Legalization/Amnesty program for Catholic Community Services. The office staff has done a tremendous job in serving more than 5,000 applicants. The program ends November 30, and on Sunday a welcome and appreciation is planned at the St. Augustine Cathedral, 192 South Stone Avenue, at 2 p.m. The public is welcome.

Now I want to tell you about the upcoming Mexican Food Cook-Off. First, some background: On December 12, 1986, the then-mayor of Tucson, Lewis C. Murphy, proclaimed Tucson the "Mexican Food Capital of the World and Elsewhere." Subsequently a cook-off was held at the Arizona Inn and the mayor challenged other towns. The following year, the contest was held at the Doubletree Hotel. Santa Fe, New Mexico took first prize and Tucson finished fourth, behind Phoenix and Albuquerque, New Mexico.

To make matters worse, on a later plane trip to some convention our new mayor, Tom Volgy, sat next to Sam Pick, the mayor of Santa Fe. Mayor Pick bragged continuously about his city's cooking. Frankly it cannot compare with ours. Our mayor decided we could not take this sitting down, not even at the dinner table, so he formed a cook-off committee. He joined forces with the Mayor of South Tucson, Victor E. Soltero, and included Pima County by asking Supervisor Dan Eckstrom to serve with them.

To reflect our entire area, they are referring to this delicious project as *El Orgullo del Valle de Tucson*, or the "The Pride of the Tucson Valley." The first contest is scheduled for Saturday, September 17, at Tucson Greyhound Park. Tickets are on sale at both of the mayors' offices, the Metropolitan Tucson Convention and Visitors Bureau, 130 South Scott Avenue, and the Greyhound Park, 2601 South Third Avenue. Any profits from the event will go to the Community Food Bank. There is a limited seating capacity for tasting all of this prize-winning food, so if you want to get your licks in, do not wait.

The second contest along with prizes is open to individuals not associated with restaurants is taking place the next day. Among our esteemed judges is Sylviana Wood, known to the Hispanic population as Doña Chona. She lets us know via radio and television about important happenings in the Old Pueblo. This cook-off is being held in conjunction with the Mexican Independence or *Fiestas Patrias* at Kennedy Park on Sunday September 18.

*Con el favor de Dios*, I will be busy eating at both events. I hope to see you there. *Hasta la vista*.

# New Book Portrays Barrios Sensitively

On Saturday a precious book entitled *Days of Plenty, Days of Want* by Patricia Preciado Martin will make its debut at the Fremont House.

The house, Casa del Gobernador, is also referred to as the Carrillo Sosa House in the Hispanic community and is the only house that was saved from urban renewal and construction of the Tucson Convention Center.

It is most appropriate that this book, which reflects that area and that era, becomes available to the general public in the place which gave it birth.

Martin was born in Prescott, but has lived most of her life in Tucson. The barrios and its people are well and sensitively portrayed in her collection of

**2F    Tucson Citizen    Tuesday, December 6, 1988**

## New book portrays barrios sensitively

On Saturday a precious little book entitled "Days of Plenty Days of Want" by Patricia Preciado Martin will make its debut at the Fremont House.

The house, Casa del Gobernador, is also referred to as the Carrillo Sosa House in the Hispanic community and is the only house that was saved from urban renewal and construction of the Tucson Convention Center.

Alva B. Torres

FIGURE 5.1 After returning, Alva updated her photograph. *Citizen*, December 6, 1988, p.2F.

eight heartwarming stories that comprise the skillfully written book. Each story has a personal, intimate touch and although the stories are written in English, Spanish words and phrases are interspersed at the appropriate time. They convey a reality that existed and still exists among the Mexican American community, that of primarily being an American with a Mexican spirit for life. She captures this wonderfully, and artistically.

I am looking forward to future writings, particularly covering the barrios and their people, as she has captured the essence magnificently in her writing. Congratulations, *felicidades*, and continued success to you, *amiga*.

# 1989

# El Tucsonense had Long Community Ties

When riding around in Tucson's downtown areas it is becoming more and more difficult to find either a building or a business I can remember that still exists from those carefree and happy years of my childhood. My heart gets mellow when I see a building, one in which the same family still does business, just as it did prior to my early childhood. Such is the building at the corner of South Stone Avenue and East McCormick Street, where I grew up. It now houses the Old Pueblo Printers, which was begun in 1966 by Albert Moreno Elías. It used to house *El Tucsonense*, a Spanish language newspaper. Albert is a grandson of the original founder of the newspaper.

In my younger days, manager Arturo Moreno used to discard a lot of silver-colored metal plates and Julietita, my little sister, and I would pretend that we were miners who had struck it rich every time there was a lot of "silver" piled behind the tin shed in the adjoining property. At that time, *El Tucsonense* was *el periodico*, referred to simply by our Spanish-speaking residents as THE newspaper. It was founded by Francisco S. Moreno in 1915. Albert tells me that Francisco was an employee of both the *Arizona Daily Star* and the *Citizen* for many years prior to that.

The first building to house *El Tucsonense* was on 0 block on South Church. Then it moved to the area where La Placita Village has its parking garage. Finally, in 1923, it was located at 255 South Stone Avenue, where it has remained. "Francisco continued publishing the paper until his untimely death at the age of 52 in 1929," said Albert. His grandmother, Rosa Elías de Moreno, then became the proprietor. They had had five children and their four sons used to be at the business every day after school to help. That is probably why they all became printers. Her eldest son, Gilbert, became the manager when his father died. The youngest son, Elías Moreno, followed him in the job.

FIGURE 6.1 *El Tucsonense* building in the 1920s at 255 South Stone Avenue. Lydia R. Otero Collection.

Elías was most active in the community and was a candidate for the City Council, running on the Republican ticket in 1939. The very week of the election his appendix ruptured and because he was so caught up in the campaign he would not stop to take care of his health. Consequently, he died that week. He was 39.

The remaining sons, Gilbert, Fred and Arthur, continued to work together at the paper. It was distributed Mondays, Wednesdays and Fridays. *El Tucsonense* has never been replaced in the Mexican community by another totally Spanish newspaper. It was always available on a subscription basis and in its earlier days it was also sold on street corners. A certain kind of bond existed between those people who read it and they used it to communicate with each other. It was as if there was a *pueblito* within the Old Pueblo. *Hasta la vista.*

# A Social Club Grows from Roots of Others

I want to transport you back in time to the late 1930s and early 1940s in the Old Pueblo. Those were the decades when clubs were prevalent in the Hispanic community.

In the 1940s the All Around Club had its beginning at Tucson High. It was made up of young women of Mexican heritage from Tucson. These girls had attended Safford Junior High and had shared friendships for years. Some of them remember a predecessor club called HCC for "Ha Cha Chas" and wanted to form their own club. They decided to get together and form a social club to hold parties, picnics and Mother-Daughter lunches and at the same time raise money for charitable causes. Their good times included a lot of singing together in their respective homes and churches as well as picnics at el Canyon de Sabino, ranchos, and Monte Limon [Mount Lemmon].

But most of all they remember *Las Fiesta Patrias* on September 16. And they always remember their dances, first at the old Blue Moon and later at El Conquistador, the Pioneer and the Santa Rita hotels and the American Legion. When all of the members had graduated from Tucson High, this came to an end—but their memories live on.

Although some of the members continued to see each other for a while, as time went by and Tucson grew they went off in different directions, most of them into marriage. None of this in itself is unusual. What is different is that in June 1981, Eduardo, known to all his friends as Lalo Guerrero (a successful singer and songwriter) and his wife, Lydia, paid a visit to Tucson. They had a get-together with their old school chums. All of them enjoyed themselves so much that some of the members of the former clubs, led by Genevieve Martinez Whalen, decided to regroup and take up where they left off so many years before. This time the group called itself Club Recuerdo (*recordar* means to remember).

They not only remember the good times, but they are having a wonderful time "building new memories" and giving their children the opportunity to be a part of this by including them in their festivities. Besides holding private activities, Club Recuerdo shares its fun by holding three *tardeadas* a year. These dances are held *en la tarde*, or afternoon. Every time they hold these dances they designate the profits to a specific charity. Among the past recipients are La Frontera, St. Elizabeth of Hungary Clinic, Boy Scouts of America, the Legalization Amnesty Program, as well as the Community Food Bank and Santa Cruz Church. This time the profits are to go for scholarships at Tucson High School, their alma mater. They have given out more than $10,000 in the last few years and built many good recuerdos at the same time.

All of you are invited to join Club Recuerdo and the dance band Los Classix and dance to music from the fabulous '30s and '40s. This tardeada is to be held at the Holidome-Holiday Inn, 4550 South Palo Verde Blvd. on Sunday from 2–6 p.m. There will be a dance contest with prizes. Cost is $8 per person. *Están todos cordialmente invitados.* Do not be shy about joining us. When you introduce yourself to me, I will be most happy to introduce you to all the members, including a former *16 de Septiembre reyna* (beauty queen), now the president of the club (Bernice Ortiz), and the newest members (Natalia Benites and Evelina Venturo). For further information call Olivia Arriaga at 623-XXXX or Hope Cervantes at 326-XXXX. I hope to see you there. *Hasta la vista.*

# El Cine Plaza Alive in Fond Memories

Let's go on a memory trip to El Cine Plaza (Plaza Theater), the Tucson theater that helped transport us by means of Spanish-language films to Mexico and other parts of Latin America.

El Cine Plaza, which was at 132 West Congress Street, was built in 1929 and survived until 1969, when it became a victim of downtown urban renewal. It was owned originally by Aaron Kaufman. It had a seating capacity of 650 and the best acoustics, ventilation, heating and cooling for the times. It also had the latest movie equipment. Local architect Roy Place designed it with a Spanish motif that included a tiled tower. It was a good-looking building, as I recall.

Kaufman knew little about theaters and wanted to lease it out, so he talked to B.H. Solot, who at that time represented Tucson Realty and Trust. Solot handled the lease, and it was taken over by Joe Gross, an operator from Los Angeles. Its grand opening was July 3, 1930, but it closed within a year and a half.

Tucsonan "Georgie" Diamos, as my father affectionately calls him, was in the theater business and wanted to pick up the lease, but he did not want anyone to know about it. Diamos went to Los Angeles (L.A.) and wired Kaufman. He said something like, "I would appreciate you meeting me in L.A. on a very important matter." Kaufman took the next train to L.A. and they made a deal.

The first thing Diamos did was to build an inside lobby. Before, when a patron walked into the theater from the outside lobby (where the cashier was located), they stepped directly into the theater. The new grand opening was held on July 4, 1932, and it was a great success.

FIGURE 6.2  Plaza Theater in 1968. Courtesy Special Collections, University of Arizona Library.

Obtaining films from Mexico was not easy, and it was not until Rafael Calderón, from Mexico who had been involved in promoting vaudeville, provided Diamos a steady source of films. He formed Azteca Studios in Mexico City and they formed a connection that brought 30 or 40 films from Mexico per year to El Cine Plaza. In 1936, Diamos was able to add to the Mexican film lineup when the Clasa-Momhe Studio was formed in Mexico. Still, El Cine Plaza didn't become solely a theater for Spanish-language films until the late 1940s. Diamos had also been able to acquire some films from Argentina, but most of the Mexican patrons were not too crazy about those because, "Ellos hablan el español muy estraño" (They speak Spanish real funny).

I believe all Mexican Americans and other Spanish-speaking people who lived in Tucson went to El Cine Plaza sometime during the 1930s and 1940s, and for sure when Mario Moreno played the insufferable comedian Cantinflas. Many of us went there frequently. I recall that the patrons usually tolerated babies in the theater, but my mother says that once she was very gently and politely requested to leave with a screaming child. She was given a free pass to return. This was the exception. Entire families attended from newborn babies, to *abuelitos* and *niños*. El Cine Plaza was a family affair.

I never fully realized until I grew up that it was at the Plaza where I met Carmen Amaya [Spanish flamingo dancer] in a film. It was also at the Plaza where I learned songs such as "La Feria de las Flores" from a movie of the same name. It was at the Plaza where I sang along with Jorge Negrete or Pedro Infante, who was a favorite of a lot of the girls. I loved to hear Toña La Negra sing and my favorite singer was and is still Pedro Vargas.

El Cine Plaza not only gave me the opportunity to "live" in Mexico, but it made my living in Tucson very special. Even though I was still here in Tucson, I was also a part of all the Mexican *ferias, sierras, ríos, iglesias, conventos, cantianas, casas, ranchos* and *familias* we saw on the screen. To a child, the big screen was something we could get lost in and become a part of. I will continue this memory trip with you next week. *Hasta la vista.*

# La Casa Cordova is Important to Save

The *Citizen* has begun publishing on Mondays a series of important articles titled "Our Forgotten Past." After I read the first installment on May 29, I was especially sad, as a person of Mexican descent, to be reminded that so much of our past has been ignored or forgotten.

One of the places still standing that was located in the Old Presidio downtown is the building called La Casa Cordova. When the Tucson Museum of Art (TMA) was being planned for the downtown area in 1970, many people objected because it involved knocking down the oldest part of La Casa Cordova, built in 1863 within the walled Presidio.

Prior to that time, letters from the Tucson-Pima County Historical Commission had been sent to the planners with detailed explanations of the importance of the structure. Therefore, when the plans were unveiled there was no excuse for ignoring La Casa. But through the help of many people—of all ethnic backgrounds and financial strata—the powers that be were finally convinced that the Casa should be saved. The plans were redrawn and Casa Cordova was included.

Unfortunately, the museum, now strapped by budget deficits, has closed the Casa because of a lack of funds.* The Art Center Block, of which La Casa Cordova is a part, is leased to the TMA for a dollar a year by the City of Tucson. I translate this to mean that all the citizens of Tucson are contributing to the subsidizing of this institution. Probably some of our visitors also contribute.

---

*The TMA ended up closing La Casa Cordova for renovations in 1989. They opened up a few rooms later that year, but initiated a pattern of sporadically closing and shortening hours when visitors could have access to La Casa. In 2017, they installed an exhibit in the house and staged a more formal reopening.

If those of Mexican de-
scent in this community had
been advised about this closing of La Casa, I believe we
would have tried to help. We
do not want to see a site built
in the presidio era be allowed
to die of apathy by those who
should know better and who
have the power to try to do
something about it. I cannot
in good conscience remain
silent when something so

FIGURE 6.3  La Casa Cordova at 175 North Meyer Avenue in 2016. Courtesy of prentiss wolfe.

important is being allowed to disintegrate before our eyes. I do not believe
there was, or is, a conspiracy to obliterate the sites that mark Tucson's Indian
or Hispanic heritage. I also believe that those in charge at City Hall did not
have the background, either in the history of the Southwest or of the world
in general, to place a real value on these priceless sites.

It is sad but true, to many people the word "progress" also seems to mean
"destroy." It is as if someone had looked at every building that had true aes-
thetic or historical value to Tucson and said: "Blast that down . . . Blow it to
smithereens . . . Disintegrate it." Just look at what we—even in our lifetime—
have seen destroyed, regardless of its importance. To see the El Conquistador and that beautiful, palm-lined drive disappear was a sad day. To see the
mezzanine at the Santa Rita Hotel, fall to bulldozers was another one. The
Jacobs house, the Otero house—in fact, all of the area where La Placita stands
downtown. Keeping this old section of Tucson would have allowed us to rival
Old Town in San Diego or Albuquerque, New Mexico.

We have lacked vision and heart. We should at least look into the little
that is left, and that sets Tucson apart as a wonderful old place, the spring at
the foot of the black mountain. Look into, and take some time to remember,
all those that went on before us, what they did, what they built, making it
possible for us to be here now. Be proud of what we had and still have.

# Mike the Gas Man has 84th Birthday

First of all, Feliz Cumpleaños to my father, Miguel Bustamante N., who is celebrating his 84th birthday. For many years he was well-known in the Old Pueblo as THE Gas Man.

Dad began working in the gas business in 1927 and started his own business in 1944. He named it Gas Equipment Service. The business was run out of our home on McCormick Street. We later moved to 1228 East 12th Street.

He started the entire operation with a $600 loan (no collateral), from P.J. Solomon, owner of the then well-known Star Outfitters on South Meyer Avenue. The only things Dad had back then was his own set of tools from his employment at Hearn and Caid Heating and Cooling, and many satisfied customers. With the borrowed capital, Dad bought a little, used van and had it lettered with his name, the company name and the telephone number. Later he listed his business in the Yellow Pages.* Mama was instantly drafted to be his secretary and office manager.

During that first summer some days would pass without a call, so he decided to work on evaporative coolers as well as gas appliances, but it was the latter in which he excelled. During World War II he would build parts when none were available and repair things that other people would have thrown out. His reputation grew to the point that he eventually had to turn down new customers and stop advertising. During season changes some customers would wait for weeks to have the heating or cooling changed over, as long as he did their work. He had a reputation for knowing his work well and being honest. He never wanted to sell appliances because he felt it might become too easy to sell, instead of repair, which at that time was more economical.

---

*Miguel Navarro Bustamante opened Gas Equipment Service in 1941.

At first, all of his business either came by word of mouth or through his old customers searching him out.

Until he retired 50 years later, he never once had an accident that jeopardized a customer or property, nor did he ever have a dissatisfied customer. No matter what time Dad was called to go to a customer who had a dangerous situation, he always responded. Dad was asked to go as far as Flagstaff to see about fixing gas appliances, but declined because he had more than he could handle right here in southern Arizona and even across the border. He had plenty of elderly customers and would always go out of his way for them. He would also go out of his way for sick or recovering patients or a mother coming home with a new baby who needed the heat turned on when it suddenly got cold or the cooling when it was exceptionally hot. He would get to know all of his customers personally. Sometimes Dad would lower a fee for someone in financial trouble or take payments on time, before it became common. Although Dad had a number of different men work for him over the years, some customers wanted nobody but Mike the Gas Man. Dad served most of the restaurants in town and did some work for some of the restaurant chains.

We finally talked Dad into retiring when he was 72. We did not want him climbing up on the rooftops any more. After that he became more active in community organizations, his favorite being the South Tucson Lions Club. Last year he was the club's top raffle salesman. No matter where he went, who he was with or what the occasion, he sold tickets. In fact, he spent every Saturday at one mall or another looking for customers. Whether it was a wedding or a funeral, no matter, out came the ticket book. And he also helped in all of their other activities.

A couple of months ago he decided to stay closer to home with Mama. One thing my parents still have is our old O'Keefe and Merritt gas stove. It looks spotless, works wonderfully and cooks as well as any newfangled model. It is still my favorite cooking appliance. Just like Dad, it's looking good, is reliable and effective. It has character and is still cooking with gas. *Hasta la vista.*

# Leyla Cattan Informs Hispanic Community

Today my column is about a very fine lady from Panama who arrived here in 1968. Leyla Cattan immediately became an important asset to the Hispanic community.

When she arrived in Tucson she was concerned about the lack of written information available to Spanish-speaking people. She wrote a Spanish-language column for the University of Arizona newspaper, the *Wildcat*, in 1968 and 1969. By 1970, Cattan and Raul Gamez were producing a television news segment called "Noticiero." In 1972 she began to write a Spanish column for the *Arizona Daily Star*. She began with one column, went on to two, and by 1980, was writing three columns a week for the newspaper. In 1973 and 1974, she also was the commentator on Channel 11 for a television program called "Movies at Home." From 1975 to 1977, she was the hostess of "Rosita's Show," a program about different aspects of Hispanic life. The same year, 1977, she began an informative program called "Ayer, Hoy, Mañana" (Yesterday, Today, Tomorrow). It has proved to be a very popular program that continues to the present day.

Cattan says, "Yo estoy enamorada de la información. Suprimo mi opinión por dar información. El periodista no todo el tiempo se usa como el caballito de bataya." Translation: "I am in love with information. I suppress my opinion in order to give information. Writing is not always used as a battle pony."

Cattan is leaving for Spain, courtesy of a Spanish government program that provides scholarships for American high school students interested in becoming Spanish teachers.

She had publicized the program last year, and as a result, 22 Tucson students—more than from any area of the United States—had applied for the program. Fourteen were accepted and the scholarship committee, to show its appreciation, arranged for her to travel to Spain.

When I first began my column on Mexican cooking in 1984 for the *Citizen*, Cattan was the first person involved in the Hispanic media to welcome me and to inform the community about my new venture. After I stopped writing my column for a while, she reintroduced me to newcomers and reminded Tucsonans that my column was once more being published. For this and for all your efforts, *muchísimas gracias*, Leyla, and may you continue to inform the Hispanic community. We love you. *Cariñosamente*, Alva. *Hasta la vista.*

# Green Corn Tamale Time is Too Short

We are now in a special time in the Old Pueblo known as "el tiempo para hacer tamales de elote," or "green corn tamale time." Those of us who love green corn tamales can only regret that they are available for what seems to be such a short time in August and September.

Here is a different recipe for green corn tamales from ones I have given you previously:

TAMALES DE ELOTE

    1 dozen ears of fresh white corn
    1½ pounds of Crisco, margarine, lard or a portion of each
    ¾ cup shredded longhorn cheese
    salt to taste
    1 pound of longhorn cheese, diced or in strips
    6 blistered and peeled green chiles, cut into strips

1. Cut off the ends of the green corn, saving the husks and then washing the husks and standing them up to dry.

2. After washing the corn thoroughly, remove the kernels.

3. Take the corn to a Mexican food store to be ground. Many stores will do this, such as La Suprema, El Zarape or Grande Tortilla Factory.

4. Beat the shortening until fluffy.

6. Add the masa (the ground corn), shredded cheese and salt and mix together.

6. Place a corn husk in one hand and put a tablespoon of the prepared masa in the center, bottom half.

7. Add a strip (or strips) of green chile and some cheese.

8. Fold one side over and then the other side over it and then fold the top down over all. Place in a standing position with open end up.

9. Place all of these in a tamale pot. Add water and cover with extra husks and steam for about 45 minutes. Allow to cool and test for doneness. If you do not have a tamale pot, place foil or a metal object on the bottom of the pot and when you pour the water into it. Make sure the tamales are standing free of the water. Otherwise you will end up with a big mess instead of tender, fluffy delicious green com tamales.

My landlady, Jesus "Chu" Flores, used to make the best tamales. She would add a bit of cottage cheese to the masa. She did not fold the tamales the way we do now; she simply placed the masa on the bottom half of the *hoja* (husk) and made the top one-fold over the bottom. She always served these with *frijolitos fritos* (fried beans) and *calabasitas* (zucchini squash, made with garlic, onions and fresh tomato). Some recipes include a teaspoon of baking powder.

If we are really lucky we might even have some late green corn and be able to sample some at the Mexican Cook-Off, "El Orgullo del Valle," coming up on October 8. But I cannot wait for even the first fiesta. I am bound to get some today, even if I have to make a few myself. *Hasta la vista.*

# *Cimmarrona* Shops Stir Old Memories

I remembered the other night that one of our old-fashioned summer treats used to be to go and get a *cimmarrona* or a *raspado*. In English this roughly translates into a Sno Cone, a forerunner of an Icee.*

There are several places in Tucson where you can find a cimmarrona or a raspado, but I am going to tell you about two them. Both of them, curiously enough, sprang from one man and the one place where we could buy cimmarronas in my childhood days.

As far back as I recall, people could walk over to La Calle Meyer and 17$^{th}$ Street to La Providencia [614 South Meyer Avenue] and buy a cool, refreshing cimmarrona for 5 cents. Literally, a cimmarrona was a wild goat from mountainous country that often ate the snow or ice for its liquid sustenance; thus the name cimmarrona, since it is made of ice particles and often includes milk flavorings. Raspado also means shaved and is another common name for a cimmarrona, which uses finely crushed or shaved ice.

La Providencia closed in 1977 when its owner, Ygnacio Gallego, died. It has opened this year under owners who are seeking to return the store to its origins. Gallego had run the place for the neighborhood, not only as a place to buy cimmarronas, but as a general store, too. He carried all types of groceries, candy and sodas, as well as bread, canned and packaged goods and other sundries.

The young men presently running the new store are hoping to make it more a cimmarrona place again. All were born and raised in the Barrio Histórico. Manuel Cota, Jose Valenzuela and Pete Santa Cruz have high hopes for their La

---

*Different spellings of cimmarronas such as cimmarronas, cimmarona and even cimmarron were used locally.

Providencia. They opened it on the Fourth of July and small toys, candy, sodas, ice cream and antiques are for sale along with many flavors of cimmarronas. Flavors include the traditional strawberry, cherry, orange, piña, melon and others, along with all kinds of *leche* (milk) combinations. They range from the most common, vanilla, to peanut butter. I tasted the leche chocolate and it was good.

Beside setting up the cimmarrona business, for the past 10 years they have been involved with restoring the La Providencia building, built in 1895. They told me that a friend [and the building's owner], Larry Sweet, got them interested in the place when they were in their early teens and that slowly they

FIGURE 6.4 Former "cimmarona" shop in South Tucson in 2021. Photo taken by Lydia R. Otero.

have been working on restoring the premises, including the corral. They also keep a big goat in the corral as a mascot. And although they make their own *leche* recipe, they buy all their goat milk (the goat is a billy goat).[*]

The building has been kept in close to original condition as possible. The shelves display old coffee can containers, a variety of pitchers and other interesting objects. They also sell piñatas, which include Superman, Spiderman and Batman, along with regular favorite dolls, clowns and popular Christmas star. They are open every day. Being able to buy cimmarronas not only brings back memories, but they're a nice way to ease the heat of summer. *Hasta la vista.*

---

[*]This effort to revive La Providencia and sell *cimmarronas* was sort lived and closed within a year.

# Beating Heat in the Old Pueblo

I was recently thinking about how we kept cool in the old days and weathered the summers here during my childhood in the Old Pueblo.

Many of our homes were made of thick adobe walls, which provided good insulation. They also had wonderfully large, low windows that a 5-year-old child could easily use as a door. They created a nice cross breeze. These homes were built B.C. (Before Coolers).

Most homes were positioned so they could keep their inhabitants cool. On the west side of the houses, windows were minimal or altogether missing and porches were attached to the walls, cutting down the intense afternoon sun rays. Whenever possible, trees or vines were planted both east and west. Second, we followed what I call a summer schedule, very different from the winter or school schedule. During the time we attended classes we went to bed early, rose early and led a pretty normal routine. As soon as classes let out and until after Labor Day, it was a summer schedule and I loved what I perceived as the grown-up life.

We would get up very early and do our chores until noon. Then we had a good, long meal. As soon as the dishes were washed, dried and put away, we had that midday rest known as *la siesta*. Some people slept during la siesta, which is what we were supposed to do. But if we rested and let the others rest, that was okay, too. I used to take my siesta at the Torreses. They were our next-door, downstairs neighbors. Wilma Torres; Julietita, my sister; myself and any other girls from the neighborhood would lie down in the living room on the rug with our special pillows and listen to the radio. We always listened to Stella Dallas to try to find out if "a girl from a little mining town in the West could find happiness with a noble and titled English man." (I wondered if she could not, who could?)

FIGURE 6.5 In this 1942 or 1943 photograph, Alva is on the front right, next to her sister Julieta on her left. At the top left, is family friend Aurelia Macias, next is Carmen Bustamante (Alva's mother) who is holding her daughter, Esther. Standing behind Alva is her neighbor and future mother-in-law, Teresa Acevedo Torres. Courtesy Alva B. Torres.

After our siesta, we would get up and take a nice cool shower and get dressed for dinner. Dinner itself was not too important, but as soon as those dishes were taken care of we would get together with the neighbors. Adults and kids often played together in the empty lot at McCormick Street and Scott Avenue. Later, the grown-ups would sit down and chat. If the conversation was very interesting or if they started singing, the kids that felt like it would join the grown-ups.

Often company would come over from other barrios. Then, father would tell me to run up for the lemonade or tea or whatever beverage mother had prepared. The Torres family provided the ice and glasses. Sometimes our company would bring a watermelon.

We were allowed to stay up late as we were supposed to have had a long siesta. When it was time to go to bed, we took another quick shower. This time we did not bother to dry; instead we would just slip into our loose cotton nightgowns. This kept us cool long enough to barely dry as we fell asleep under a starlit or moonlit night, dreaming of our upcoming vacations to Mexico and California. Julietita and I had our bed in one of two places, either out on the roof of the tin shed downstairs, or else sticking halfway out the balcony. Mother, father and Esthersita slept inside, in the Arizona porch.

We spent all of our spare time in one of the two refrigerated places in Tucson we knew about, the movies or the library. Of the movie houses, all five were located nearby on Congress Street, and the Carnegie Library was close to our home. We visited both of them frequently and besides keeping cool, learned a lot. But our very favorite way of keeping cool was to run outside right after a big *chubasco* (a downpour of rain) and play in the water. That beat everything else. May God bless us with many more this summer. *Hasta la vista.*

# Family, Healthcare Julia Soto's Passions

When I tried to get information from Julia Soto about herself, she talked instead about her children's accomplishments and family situations and how they handled them. Her family is her first love.

But Julia Soto's *familia* includes more than just her children Terry, Tina, Gloria, Frank Jr., Tim, Martin and Fred. It reaches to her clients and patients at El Rio Santa Cruz Neighborhood Health Center, 839 West Congress Street. Soto is director of patient services and advocacy at the center. "My interest has been in health care," she said. "I believe it is the right of every American to have health care."

Her own story began on February 16, 1930, when she was delivered by her older brother, Roberto Corral because the doctor was late. She, however, was on time. She was one of nine children. During the Great Depression she was placed at the Preventorium, where doctors tried to prevent hunger and sickness. When things got a little better she came home and attended Carrillo Elementary School and then Safford and Roskruge junior highs. Although she never graduated from high school, she thoroughly believes in a good education. She went back to get her General Educational Development certificate and has attended Pima Community College and the University of Arizona.

"*La educación* also should include common sense and *corazón* (heart)," she said. "We should strive for a diploma, but we should temper this with heart and using our logic. I attend seminars and always learn new things, at least two. Being able to help people solve their problems is very important. Sometimes nothing is needed but a word, a gesture or sometimes material help. Here at El Rio the biggest challenge is that people do not have the basic things like good health and education."

She went on to say that nowadays "poverty is totally different from when we were children. We have become a richer America, but in some ways, we are poorer. In the old days, people banded together to help however we could. You never saw a homeless Mexican when I was a child. Someone would take him in and make things stretch. No matter what we had, we shared it."

She said she would like to see national health insurance program instituted, based on a sliding fee scale. "I am not worried about myself," she said and shared that:

> In fact, in 19 years I have only missed a period of three days twice for flus and two weeks when I had an accident. And here I am in the clinic exposed to all kinds of sickness . . . What we deal with here is crisis medicine, it is never prevention. What this city needs is prevention. Yearly checkups and mammograms and that type of thing is what I would like to see. Children deserve good checkups. Even before that, we need good prenatal and postnatal care. El Rio Clinic is involved with a lot and Mr. (Robert) Gomez, our director, is always looking for special groups that need special health.

We shared mutual thought on the elderly. We spoke of how they have all given to this community and this country, working hard, paying their dues. No one set up special clinics to help them, those who helped build this country, and now because of inflation and longevity many of their needs are out of reach. She continued to say that children and our elderly were her main priorities when it comes to health acre.

She then wanted to tell me about her daughter, Terry. "I would rather you write about her than me. Since the time she was 16, she worked her way and up through the University of Arizona. In 1970 she received her degree in business and public administration, and every semester she pays scholarship in New Start to help other kids climb the ladder. She is *muy trabadora* (very hard-working) and is always wanting to put something from herself into our community."

Then she told me that she would like it if I would talk to Dr. Agosto Ortiz, who works with the Phoenix Health Network for Campesinos. I told her I would certainly like to meet him but that this article was about Julia Soto, a woman with a ready grin and a patient heart. It is about Julia Soto because she is someone who gives of herself to this community—especially to the Hispanic elderly who have confidence in El Rio and *confianza* to ask her about all those things they do not feel like talking about with anyone else.

One of her favorite sayings is, "*Lo bonito qué tiene la gente Mexicana* (How beautiful the Mexican people can be). We still have a great sense of familia."

# 1990

# Torres' Living Room is Now a Movie Star

A scene from the movie "Young Guns II" was filmed at my home [334 South 6th Avenue] last week. If I did not have an appreciation for all the time, energy and talent that go into filming a movie before this, I sure do now.

To begin with, my dining and living rooms were transformed completely. Not only was all of my furniture removed, the walls and windows were changed, as well as the lighting, for the film. The film is set in 1891 in Santa Fe, New Mexico. My family and I had a great time watching the transformation to that time period. My granddaughters, Shenoa and Jacquay, were most thrilled with meeting two of the stars, Emilio Estevez and Lou Diamond Phillips. Both were *amables* (gracious) and down to earth, as were all of the people involved.

Each one knew his or her business and did it quickly and efficiently. Teamwork was evident from early morning until late evening. They brought their own dressing studios, commodes, equipment and caterers. One member of the "friendly army" had a shirt that said, "Every day we make it, we'll make it the best we can." The house seemed even more

## ● A little army

**Alva Torres** has had what she calls a "friendly invasion" in her South Sixth Avenue home.

For two days this week, the Tucsonan's house was taken over by the stars and staff of "Young Guns II" for filming of some movie scenes.

"It's like having an army in there," Torres says. "There were about 70 people in the house, but they've been very cordial, very careful."

Though Torres has turned over her house to the film crew, she's not interested in getting herself in the movie.

"The last thing I want to do is be a movie star," she says. "Or maybe the last thing would be a politician . . ."

FIGURE 7.1 Announcement. *Citizen*, January 20, 1990, p.1B.

FIGURE 7.2  2006 photo of Alva's former home at 334 South 6th
Avenue where filming took place. Lydia R. Otero Collection.


unreal when the windows were covered with black material and the porch
was draped from top to bottom to simulate night. Then to go outside and
see snow everywhere on the day of the shooting transported me to another
place and era. I have not seen "Young Guns" yet, but I intend to see it and,
of course, to see this sequel.

# Easter Traditions Easy to Find Here

Easter Sunday, or Pascua, is just around the corner. If you can, try to see the Yoeme (Yaqui) celebrations this week.

I remember Daddy taking us to Old Pascua, when there was only one Pascua Village, during Holy Week to see the men perform. Even then it seemed something strange and from another time and place. And, of course, it is.

Another event that has become traditional in Tucson, and which is now in its 20th year, was begun by our own David Herrera. He organized a group of men called Los Dorados. They carry a large cross up the road on Sentinel Peak, commonly called A Mountain, on Good Friday (*Viernes Santo*). Besides organizing the entire event and repainting the cross himself, each year David and others hold a vigil on both Friday and Saturday night. On Sunday morning at 6 a.m., a sunrise Mass is held at the site at which the cross is set. Many Tucsonans and visitors, along with mariachi musicians, welcome the sunrise with song and praise. It is a beautiful event and we congratulate David for all his years of caring and unselfish service to this community, for many contributions, and most especially for this spiritual event attended by devoted Hispanic, Chicano and Mexican American people.

When we were children it was common for families to celebrate this Holy Day by going to picnics after attending church services. We did not do this but we knew others who did. Instead, Mother sewed us new Easter dresses and we went to Myerson's White House to get our new, white Easter Sunday shoes. Some of you might recall that in those days, they had a machine we would slip our feet into to see how the shoes fit. I think about it now and then and wonder if any ill effects will show up. It appeared to be a fluo-

Smart, smooth lines combine with concealed comfort features to make Natural Bridge Shoes today's popular choice. Women everywhere admire their soft, fine leathers, their superb craftsmanship and their easy-going comfort.

**Smart Elasticized Bow Pump Underlaid Perforation on Vamp**
Navy Blue
Black
White

9.95

Smarter Shoes for Natural Walking

X-RAY FITTING

*Myerson's White House Department Store*

the store of MASTER FITTERS

FIGURE 7.3 Advertisement. *Citizen*, March 20, 1949, p.16.

rescent or X-ray picture, showing our bones and the shoes.* Anyway, we also would get new, fancy white socks to go with our shoes. Besides this, Mother also bought us Easter bonnets and new purses. I could not imagine wanting to go on a picnic. Instead, I wanted to parade in my new clothes.

Mother and Father also had Easter outfits and Mama had the most beautiful hats. She was fond of large picture hats. Her favorite color was black. These were adorned with either ribbons or flowers or both. Teresita Torres, who later became my mother-in-law and was our next-door downstairs neighbor, along with her daughters, also always had hats. One year my mother and Teresita (now often called Nani) both bought identical hats. Nobody knew ·until Easter Sunday and when they did, they both laughed.

Another time, they both chose the same rug and, when I was getting married to Alberto Torres, both of them, unbeknownst to anyone, gave me identical perfume gold filigree bottles. They loved much the same things and had very similar tastes. This made life much easier after Alberto and I were married. In all the years we have known each other, 54, a cross word has never been said. Besides that, they both now are great-grandmothers to some of the

---

*A few other local stores such as Sears, Roebuck and Co and Given Shoes also advertised x-ray fluoroscope machines that ensured customers a good-fitting shoe by x-raying their feet.

same children and share their love together. They are both, thank God, still with us and just that makes everything extra special.

May your Easter Sunday be a most beautiful one and I wish on you the spirit of this spring season and the spirit of youth, rebirth and love. God bless you. *Cariñosamente.* Happy Easter and Happy Passover.

# Mariachi Conference Brings Joy, Pride

Last weekend was a most memorable one for Tucsonans, especially Hispanics, and one that brought us a lot of joy and pride. Tucson hosted the eighth annual Mariachi Conference. One of the purposes of the conference is to allow young mariachi students, ages 10 to 15, the opportunity to take lessons from the famous Mariachi Vargas de Tecalitan of Mexico, from Mariachi Los Camperos de Nati Cano of California, and Tucson's own Mariachi Cobre, now based in Florida. This year, more than 400 students received instruction.

Besides this, they also put on a wonderful program at the Tucson Convention Center for the benefit of La Frontera Center. Last year many fans were shut out and disappointed when the program's only performance was a sellout, so this year they added a matinee. At the rate they are attracting new fans, it will soon require another performance. I have been able to attend all of them and it is gratifying to see this become so successful. Linda Ronstadt was better than ever. Busloads of people came in from California and Texas and carloads from everywhere else, including Sonora and Sinaloa, Mexico.

Another event of this conference is Garabaldi Night. All the musicians play for *el pueblo*. This year they set up an extra platform at East 14th Street and South Sixth Avenue. The main stage was in the stationary shell in Armory Park. Musicians were having as much fun as the huge crowd at Armory Park. And the thousands sitting and standing joined in singing when they played *Volver, Volver, Volver*.

Mariachi Cobre also played for a special Saturday morning Mass at the *Catedral San Augustine*. Its members did not appear the least bit tired and gave a long, enthusiastic free concert to the friendly crowd which always waits for them. Some of these boys were in the original *Changuitos Feos* and have inspired others to follow them. Randy Carrillo is their director and he is excellent.

An important part of Garabaldi Night is the food, which is homemade and served out of decorated booths. Although there were at least 36 *puestos* (booths), they were not prepared for the influx of people who strolled South Sixth Avenue between the old library and Armory Park. After the

FIGURE 7.4 Fiesta at Armory Park. Courtesy Special Collections, University of Arizona Library.

Saturday matinee let out, one Tucson police officer on duty estimated that at least 6,000 people showed up all at the same time. He also guess-timated that, at its peak, about 25,000 people were at the park, listening to music and forming long lines waiting for food. Some of the booths simply had to close when they ran out of food; others started improvising. I am sure they will be better-prepared next year.

On Sunday afternoon El Mariachi Cobre again played at *la Catedral*, this time for persons from around the world attending the National Association for Bilingual Education conference here. The Mass was bilingual. Steve Carrillo beautifully sang "Ave Maria," which was most moving. They all received a big thank you from Bishop Moreno and a big round of applause from the audience. After Mass, many photos were snapped and *muchos abrazos*, lots of hugs, were received from friends and relatives for the mariachis. *Hasta la vista*.

# Family Grocery Store Starts Tortilla Empire

One of the best-smelling grocery stores in town is in Barrio Anita on North Anita Avenue, behind the Davis Bilingual Learning Center.

There, Mario Lopez Soto and his wife, Grace Flores de Soto, opened their new business on February 19, 1984. It all started when Mario, who is in construction, was repairing the grocery store. The owner asked him if he and his wife would be interested in renting the place. Mario talked it over with Grace, who had worked in the kitchen of the Arizona Children's Home for seven years. Her family had also run a grocery store in Nogales, Sonora, for several years.

Grace was reluctant, but her husband convinced her that they should "*hacer la lucha*," or give it a try. "But then we started and, thanks be to God, things have gone well," Grace said. The reason things are going well is because they began to make tortillas two years ago for the burritos that they sold there. At first, they made four or maybe five dozen large flour tortillas daily. At last count, they were up to more than 200 dozen daily. After a short time, they added what they call "*gorditas*." These are smaller flour tortillas that contain more shortening than the regular ones. And, just recently, they have added corn tortillas to their list of offerings, and those also are selling well. Besides tortillas, they also sell *carne de chile colorado*, or meat in red chile. They also prepare their own *carne seca*, referred to as jerky.

The Sotos run the grocery store and do the cooking themselves, with only one helper. Their tortillas are good and taste homemade. I know some women who usually make their own but who also run out and buy some from the store when they just don't have time to *tortillar*, or pat the tortillas out. Neither their family nor friends can tell the difference. After everyone has eaten, the women laugh and confess, "Everyone who comes in and buys a dozen of our tortillas, as soon as they taste them, becomes our client. But we work hard," Grace said. Mario told me he experimented until he found the perfect recipe.

The Sotos have five children, who range in age from 19 to 30, and eight grandchildren. One of the grandchildren, Gracie, 4, likes to greet people and is usually at the grocery store whenever I stop by.

Besides tortillas, the Sotos also sell burros de carne con chile—either red or green—machaca, jerky and beans. They also sell ground beef and bean tostadas and quesadillas, which is melted cheese in a tortilla. The word "quesadillas" also refers to a very special cheese made in the form and size of corn tortillas. The couple also sell Mexican pastries, such as *pan de huevo, coyotas, chochitos and yo yos.* They also sell basic items, along with candy, gum, sodas, small Mexican paperback books and an array of herbs.

Grace said that she and her husband are enjoying their new venture. As a satisfied customer, I am glad they went into it. The store is at 849 North Anita Avenue, in Barrio Anita, a well-known Mexican barrio. Many people are finding themselves there again, just to buy tortillas. *Hasta la vista.*

# Tucson's First Black Dentist Reminisces

Dr. Floyd Thompson was the first black dentist to hang his shingle in Tucson. He was my dentist until he retired a few years back. I had not seen the doctor for years and thought a column about him would be interesting. According to Thompson:

"We came here in 1919, from Houston, Texas, where I was born. I attended school here and then went on to Howard University dental school in Washington, D.C. I met Nellie who was a dental hygienist—while there. I graduated in June of 1942 and we were married in December that same year. The Second World War was on and I became a first lieutenant in the Dental Corps. I was stationed at the hospital at Fort Huachuca for one year. From there I was sent to serve in Guadalcanal. *Soy veterano.* I was then reassigned to Fort Huachuca. Later I was discharged from the nearest center, which was William Beaumont General Hospital, El Paso, Texas, in January 1946."

"When I came back to my town, I had a lot of difficulty renting an office. Nobody wanted to rent to a black dentist. Finally, E.D. Herreras rented me an office on South Main. He was one of my great supporters. At that time (the rent) was $45 a month," Thompson said. "Now there are five black dentists in Tucson and two of them started practicing at *mi oficina.* You remember, I always had an integrated office staff and also patients."

Dr. Thompson's Spanish was good even then. When did he learn to speak it? "When I was just a little kid, living in the barrio, playing with the little *Mejicanitos,* one thing I could not understand then was why I could not go to school with them. All of the black children had to go to Dunbar, you remember. My playmates and I could not understand it." Thompson's son, Floyd Jr., could not understand it either, as his father remembered:

> Every morning I would drive him to school. We lived on *la esquina* (corner) of Cherry and 22nd. We would first pass Elizabeth Borton, and my son would ask, 'Dad, how come I can't go to that school there?' Then we would go by Safford and he would ask the same thing. If we went by Drachman and Carrillo, which were also en route, he wanted to know why he could not go there. Then when he played with his little friends near the house, they had the same question. By the time my third child went to school, the integration policy had been initiated. Before this came to pass, we had some hectic times. Mayor Don Hummel appointed an interracial committee to fight discrimination. Dr. Robert Morrow really helped.

FIGURE 7.5  A young Floyd Thompson. Courtesy of Floyd Thompson.

> I remember when a black person could not get a drink of water anywhere downtown. We had a strategy. Do you remember the old Martin Drug Store? Crede Taylor was selected to ask Andy Martin if he would allow black people to get some water there. Then Dorsey Watson was to approach the manager of Woolworth's *en la Congresso*, and I was to do the same at Walgreens, also on Congress Street. When we asked them, Mr. Martin said he was willing if the other two stores would join him. They said the same thing. These were the first three places where we could get a glass of water or a soda.

> The Pioneer Hotel, at the time was the most prestigious. We, in the dentist association, held our meetings there and also had dinner preceding the meeting. We had a gentlemen's agreement that I was to wait out in the foyer and not come in until dinner was over. Then I would go in and attend the business meeting. One evening, Dr. Paul Bennett, originally from Atlanta, saw me in the hall and asked me what I was doing there. I briefly explained. He said to

me, 'You come in right now to dinner and you are going to sit right beside me. If anybody says anything, let them tell me. Here was this dental surgeon from the South, who sat on the State Board of Examiners, doing something about discrimination. Nobody else had ever spoken up for me at those meetings.

Next week I will continue this article about Dr. Thompson. *Hasta la vista.*

# First Black Dentist Worked for Change

Last week I introduced Dr. Floyd Thompson, the first black dentist to practice in Tucson. He was our family dentist and we all remember his office on South Main, in the heart of Barrio Histórico or Barrio Viejo, as it is also called.

Thompson recalled the first three places in downtown Tucson where a black person could get a drink of water: Martin Drug Store, Woolworth Co. and Walgreen Drug Store. We continued our talk and I told him that I remember when he used to gather coloring books, crayons, toys etc., especially at Christmas time, to take out to the migrant children. I knew he went out to Marana on a regular basis for years, so I asked him about that:

"Dean Wolf, minister in Marana, called me one day and told me that some old dental equipment had been donated to their health facility there, but nobody was there to use it," Thompson said. Wolf told Thompson a dentist was needed in Marana for the Mexicans, Indians, blacks, Chinese and poor whites.

"Wolf said he would really appreciate it, but no money was available. I decided to donate half a day each Wednesday," Thompson said. "The first year, all I did was extract, *pura extracion*. Their teeth were in such bad condition. *Pobres* (Poor people). If you could have seen their teeth. After some time, the Pima County Health Department began to pay me for Wednesday afternoons and I later added another half day on Fridays."

I asked him if any of his six children had become dentists and he replied that one began but decided to go a different route. Then he very proudly told what each one was doing, and talked about his grandson, Floyd Thompson III, graduating from Pistor Middle School with honors.

He has 10 grandchildren. I asked him how many lived here and he replied, with a laugh and big grin, "Too many." He told me that Floyd Jr. is the head of affirmative action for the City of Tucson and his wife, Shirley, is head pharmacist at Kino Hospital and they have four boys.

His daughter, Jackie Thompson Douglas, finished Pima College and is now a homemaker and her husband, Charles Douglas, works for the City of Tucson in the maintenance department. They have one child. His third child, Edward, has a doctoral degree in political science from the University of Tennessee at Chattanooga and lives in Boston with his wife, Mary, who attended Tufts University and is a medical doctor. They have three children. His second daughter, Kathie Thompson, is assistant principal at Howenstine School in Tucson.* He also said he has *quatitos* (twins), and that is what made him and Nellie stop having any more, he laughed. One twin is Jeannie Thompson Harron, who is a fifth-grade teacher at Roskruge Elementary School and is married to Wade Harron. They have two girls. The other twin is James, a pharmacist at Good Samaritan Hospital, married to Annette, an obstetrician gynecologist at Good Samaritan. They live in Phoenix.

Thompson said he is a life member of the National Association for the Advancement of Colored People. He was named as man of the year by the NAACP in 1963. In 1968, when he was a trustee of Mt. Calvary Baptist Church, he was praised for his active participation and his financial support. In 1973, he also received recognition from those he helped in Marana, as a man who shared and cared. In February 1976, he was cited as an Outstanding Citizen by the Tucson Urban League.

He recalled the good teachers he had and named some who old-timers might recall: "*Te acuerdas de,* Ann Rogers, Cabot, Alice Vail, Webb, Seal, Andy Tollson and Mr. Gridly *y* Tito Flores, the pharmacist, on the corner of *Congresso* and Meyer always was proud of his Mexican heritage. *Y tu papá,* I remember people saying, 'If you got a gas leak and it can't be fixed, call Miguel.' He looked handsome with his little mustache."

Dr. Thompson emphasized that he wanted me to mention Stewart Udall for being a supporter against discrimination when being a supporter was not popular. "We had a pretty good nucleus of people back here who helped fight

---

*Howenstine High School closed in 2014.

discrimination," he said. "The main thing I remember about being a child was that I could not get a drink of water or an ice cream cone. I am glad that God has given me these years. Now I am enjoying my retirement."

When he was our *dentista*, Dr. Thompson never once made a negative statement. He never once brought up any problems, except that he wished there would be parking for the handicapped. In August, Dr. Thompson will be 76. He now spends part of each day visiting the sick and the elderly. He looks pretty much the way he did when I first saw him, friendly and smiling and speaking pocho. *Hasta a vista.*

# Saving the Barrio was Difficult Under 'Urban Removal'

When urban renewal, which ended up being known as urban removal, began in 1966, it sounded very good. The primary object was to revitalize the downtown business and residential area to the west and south of East Congress Street. That was what it was designed to do.

The mechanics were in place for city government to have access to federal monies in this revitalization. When the first plans came out, businesses were to receive a portion of the money and historically significant homes were to be incorporated into the urban renewal plan. The Mexican American population lost a priceless part of our heritage as homes and sites were indiscriminately leveled. So did our Americans of Chinese descent and our Black and Indian brothers. We not only lost businesses, buildings, homes and empty spaces, we lost the feeling of being part of one another. No longer could we shop on South Meyer Street at Star Outfitters and Kaufman's Department Store, where most of the customers were Indian, Mexican American, Afro American and cowboys of different ethnic backgrounds.

I had the good fortune when I was 15, 16 and 17 to work for both of these places. The first, Star Outfitters, was owned by Philip and Mana Solomon and their main sales lady was Theresita Acevedo Torres. They knew each customer as a friend. It was a friendly place. Long before credit came into fashion, Solomon accepted time payments. There was no interest charged and some paid as little as $1 a week. Almost everything for a family could be found there, from underwear to overcoats, from cotton dresses to white satin and lace ones to make a First Holy Communion. Men's clothes also had a wide range, including tuxedos and lounging pajamas. Whatever Star Outfitters did not have, Kaufman's did, from bolts of cloth to Stetson hats. We sold

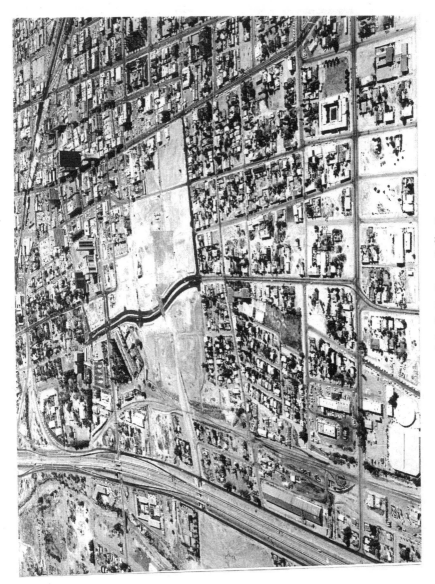

FIGURE 7.6  The devastation of urban renewal. Lydia R. Otero Collection.

a lot of boots and western shirts, and tons of Levi jeans to boys and men. Our female customers would not even dream of wearing such clothes back then.

We knew what sizes customers wore, and what they liked and went out of our way to please them. It was the same way across the street with the Diaz Pulido Brothers jewelry and clock shop. We closed up sometimes as late as 11:00 p.m. on Saturday nights and I walked home safely without a worry.

In the residential area on South Meyer Avenue, where Wild Bill Hickock stayed, I had the privilege to attend the wedding reception of Wilma and Rudy Soto. The rooms were spacious and the dining room had a bay window. Beautiful wooden floors throughout the house, perfect for dancing and having a fiesta any time, were bulldozed in the urban removal along with many other beautiful old homes. When all of this talk about urban renewal was going on, Rodolfo Soto Sr. told me, "All of our barrio and shopping area is going to disappear and nobody will even remember us old pioneers at all. Alvita, can't you try and do something to save something?" I loved Mr. Soto and his wife, Clara, and had great respect for them. The more I thought about it, the more I decided that surely, we could save *algo* (something). I walked all over the area and knew that that *algo* had to be [done to save] the Plaza de la Mesilla and its tiny kiosk (gazebo or bandshell). I wrote up a plan but nobody at city hall would talk to me, so I went to Bill Matthews at the *Arizona Daily Star*. I did not know him personally but I knew he cared about Tucson. He saw me and heard my plan and he agreed with me that the Plaza was important to save, so he wrote a letter to Don Laidlaw, then with the planning department and in charge of the urban renewal area. He told me to tell Laidlaw's secretary that I was sent by Bill Matthews.

# Reminiscing About Urban Renewal

Last week I wrote about urban renewal in Tucson, consequently called urban removal, and about some of the businesses and homes that did not survive the mid-1960s program. I also said that Rodolfo Soto Sr. inspired me to try to save the downtown Plaza de la Mesilla, now called La Placita at West Broadway and South Church Avenue.

Before I went to see Don Laidlaw at the city planning department, I went to visit Budge Painter, who was on the San Augustine Committee. The committee was interested in the area, too. At a meeting at her home that night, Painter told the committee about my ideas. Committee members Isabel Fauthauer, Gordon Leupke, Cele Peterson and Tom Price encouraged me.

When I saw Laidlaw at the city planning department, he told me there was already a plan for that [La Placita] area. I asked him if it included saving the plaza and its neighboring area, including El Charro Restaurant, the Half Moon Cafe, Zepedas Shoe Repair, The Rosequist Gallery, the Belmont Hotel, Ronquillo's Bakery, El Poblano Cafe, the Plaza Theater and a few other businesses. Adjacent to the plaza was the Menninger stone building with its tower and wonderful mezzanine, the Mariano Samaniego House built in 1881 and the Congo Bar. "Why on earth would anyone want to save the Congo Bar?" asked Laidlaw. "It is in an old building, doing good business, why not?" I replied. Then he asked me to "slay the dragon," as I called his request. He said that if I would go to each of the owners of the mentioned businesses and buildings and have them write a letter of intent to stay and acquire the funds needed to renew and revitalize their businesses, I could come back to see him.

All of the owners were interested and some gave me copies of the letters they wrote to Laidlaw. When I went back to see Laidlaw, he informed me

that there were still many obstacles to overcome if we were to save anything.
I knew the main one was that the city administration was not looking for an
Old Pueblo, but a New Pueblo. Laidlaw also said there was a new street align-
ment to be made and that East Broadway was going to merge with East Congress Street, making it impossible to save some of the buildings. I brought
along some paintings that the barber Louis Romero had done of the area and
sketches for the saving of the plaza from Victor Estrella.

At that point I decided to form a group committed to saving the plaza
and adjacent buildings. We met on a Sunday afternoon at our home on 12th
Street. Alene and Paul Smith attended, as did R. Soto Sr., his grandson Arthur
Soto, David Herrera, Ann Montaño, Viola Terrazas, Albert Montiel, Mr. and
Mrs. Ernie Esperon and E. Illiano. Later, Ernesto Portillo Sr., Joel Valdez, Fe-
lizardo Valencia, Carlitos Vasquez and Louie Barassi joined us, as did Father
Kieran McCarty and Natalia Leeney. We incorporated as the Society for the
Preservation of La Plaza de la Mesilla, but were known simply as La Placita
Committee.

We were able to gather more than 10,000 signatures, which we presented
to the Mayor and City Council, requesting the new plans integrate these old
buildings and businesses. Montiel and I appeared before the Committee on
Municipal Blight, which supported us, as did Dr. Emil Haury, Senator Dennis
DeConcini and Representative Morris Udall. Ignacio Soto from Hermosillo,
a good friend of Tucson, called a meeting at the Pioneer Hotel, where we
began meeting weekly to try and save the placita. Downtown businessmen
were invited, and Alex Jácome and others gave us their support.

In spite of all of this support, the only way we were able to save the open
space and kiosko [bandstand] was by researching the area and finding an
ordinance that deeded the plaza in perpetuity to the citizens of Tucson. Prior
to urban removal, the Tucson Festival Society had held its very popular and
successful Fiesta de la Placita at the plaza. Mexican Americans and others
had identified with this plaza since the time of the Gadsden Purchase in 1854.
We were not successful in saving the many buildings. But [the former] El
Charro, the stables and the Mariano Samaniego House still stand. The placita
has not yet regained its people, its businesses, nor its spirit. Although the kiosko no longer hosts *reynas* (queens), mariachis or fiestas, I have seen a good

number of *lindos novios*, beautiful sweethearts, joined in Holy Matrimony there. Maybe the old, new placita just needs more time.

It will never be the same, but it can still be a place where all people mingle, relax and share happy times. This is the spirit of my Old Pueblo heritage, coming together. Linked through generations by love, we all saved this placita in the heart of downtown Tucson, gracias a Dios. *Hasta la vista.*

# Ann Montaño has Made a Positive Contribution Here

When I think of Ann Montaño, I always think of a person who smiles a lot, works very hard and never complains. Outside of a handful of people and the Mexican American community, she is not well known, and yet she has had a good influence on the lives of many of our people and has made a positive impact on Tucson.

Her primary job is teaching English to non-English speakers. But just as important is her volunteer work to get people to continue their education. Every time I try to interview her, she talks of her ancestors and family— grandparents, mother, aunts and uncles, nieces and nephews. I finally told her that they each deserved a story but that I was primarily interested in knowing more about a person who had devoted herself to enhancing the educational opportunities for minorities.

Ann was born in Tucson and, as a small child, moved to Bisbee where she said she cultivated a love of nature. "I loved to run through the poppies, run through the valleys of flowers before the road was built there," she said. "My grandfather was a Spaniard who came to Nacozari, Sonora, and married an Opata Indian woman in Hermosillo. To me that is a great source of pride and I attribute my love and appreciation for nature to my Indian grandmother."

Ann was one of the first persons who was vitally interested in the quality of our drinking water and joined Tucsonans for a Clean Environment. "We have been devout in trying to interest people in the quality of our environment and in the welfare of the people of the South Side with respect to the contamination of the water," she said. Since the 1960s, she has been even more diligent in her support of the adult education program of Pima Community College. According to Edward L. Lindsey, director of the adult education program, in 1979 Ann worked with the agency as a public relations person to motivate residents of the community to take advantage of classes in English as a Second Language. She used her expertise in recruiting in the La Reforma* and in the inner-city areas. At the beginning she worked under many adverse conditions, such as holding classes in fire stations and court rooms.

For many years now, Ann has also helped Henry "Hank" Oyama, director of multi-disciplinary education and service department at Pima Community College, in motivating minorities to attend Pima. Every semester she informs the Mexican American community, through the various Spanish-language radio stations, about bilingual scholarships that are offered. She gives more than time. She is interested in helping her many students at Service Employment Redevelopment, a city and county program where she has been employed since 1971.

She has had her difficult times. In 1974 Ann had a serious medical problem that made it impossible for her to use her voice. She then had to learn to speak all over again. That year her life was saved when former Arizona Senator Barry Goldwater sent an airplane to deliver a lifesaving rare blood to Mexico City where Ann underwent an emergency operation. He also sent a plane to bring her home.

It was when we were working on La Placita Committee that I first met Ann and saw how hard she worked to try and save the area. Ann's own grandmother had to leave the home she entered as a bride and move because of urban renewal downtown. Doña Leonides Placencia Wall, Ann's grandmother, died heartbroken, forced out of her memory packed home, where she knew all of her neighbors and where she felt at ease and comfortable. Even though Ann felt sad for her grandmother, she continued to fight for others who were still close by and she joined El Tiradito Committee, founded by Rosendo Perez, who was victorious in preserving the neighborhood.

This semester she is still giving of herself at El Pueblo Neighborhood Center, encouraging potential students to continue their education. Ann is a very loving and lovely person and I admire her. *Hasta la vista.*

---

*Built after WWII, the large public housing complex known as La Reforma was located on the southern outskirts of downtown between 19th and 22nd streets in Barrio Santa Rosa. It was demolished in 1983.

# Tamales: Togetherness Just Part of the Family's Recipe

Their restaurant's name and location may have changed, but the members of this family haven't quit making delicious tamales for the past 22 years.

In 1988, Guadalupe and Luis Granillo opened a small restaurant in a tiny building on West St. Mary's Road. They called it St. Mary's Hot Tamale Factory. Although Guadalupe was born in Escuinapa, Sinaloa, Mexico, it was in another Mexican *pueblito* called La Mesa, between Imuris and Magdalena Sonora, where she learned how to make her delicious tamales.

In 1970, one of their daughters, Ana Granillo, bought the business from her parents and took over the making of the tamales. Ana's sister, Maria Jesus Salazar, helped her daily by making fresh, large flour tortillas. She brought her children to work with her. In 1982, Ana decided she did not want to run the business any longer, and she sold it to Maria Jesus's husband, Jose Luis Salazar. The business grew out of its tiny space, and in 1988 the business moved down the block, expanded its menu and changed its name. But Ana still comes over and makes their tamales.

The business now sells tacos *de birria*, rice and beans, enchiladas and burros, and oodles of green corn and chile tamales. Ana comes in about once a week to make 40 dozen of each type of tamale. The family buy the corn by the sack, shucks the leaves and then cuts the grains off the cob. This is promptly taken to the *molino* and ground into *masa*. The leaves are saved to cook the

FIGURE 7.7 St. Mary's Hot Tamale Factory at 1014 West St. Mary's Road before it expanded and moved down the block. Lydia R. Otero Collection.

tamales in and are always fresh. This gives a special flavor to the tamales, along with the fresh green chile, which is first blistered and peeled and mixed with grated yellow cheese.

There's a difference in the way Ana makes her green corn and chile tamales. With the chile tamales, she spread the chile and masa across the husk. With the green corn tamales, she sets the masa in the middle of the bottom two-thirds of the husk, then puts the chile and cheese on top of that. In both cases, she folds the tamales the same way; right side over the center, left side over both and then the top folded down over the rest. She then freezes them in large trays and cooks them during the week as needed.

I asked whether the three Salazar children want to keep up the family business and was given a big "no." But then Heriberto the youngest, who is interested is electronics and computer engineering said he just might. All of the children have been helping out the family restaurant business since they can remember. I asked the sisters how they felt about working together and helping each other. Maria Jesus and Ana smiled and said almost simultaneously: "Todo el tiempo hemos estado juntas" (We have always been together), and then they laughed.

St Mary's Mexican Restaurant is 1030 West St. Mary's Road and is open 9 a.m. to 6 p.m. Monday through Saturday.

# Tuesday

## This tree is full of special memories

Native Tucsonan Alva Torres pays tribute to a tree growing in downtown Tucson that meant a lot to her as a child and still holds a special place in her heart today. In tomorrow's Citizen.

FIGURE 7.8 Announcement. *Citizen*, October 1, 1990, p.1B.

# Tree is Playground for Child's Fantasies

Trees are very important to me. They are not showy like flowers, but I find them beautiful and admirable. Today I am sharing my special tree with you.

*Mi arbol* is not a tall and majestic or an old, old tree. It is over 50, though, and considering everything, it is a fair size. And it is a brave tree, if a tree can be called that. First of all, mi arbol was always fun to play in, around, under, and on. When I was little and it was small, it was the kind of tree a little girl could easily climb. Mi arbol was transformed into a store, a library, a church, a school, a home, a fort, a tower, an airplane or anything else my child's mind could fancy. Sometimes mi arbol was a grocery store with lots of newspaper fishes, green crayon lettuce or grapes, yellow crayon lemons and orange crayon oranges. Other times it was a special school where I could be the principal, the janitor, the teacher and the student, all on the same day.

Julieta also played in the tree, but her magic place was the Temple of Music and Art. We were not the only ones to use the tree. Albert Torres, the 11-year-old boy next door, shared it with us. He transformed it into a tower or a fort. In fact, this is where he first flirted with his future bride—me. Throwing china berries at me, but not too hard was one way to get my attention. They kind of fell on me like rain, soft and fleshy, and never left a trace. But when he threw them at the neighborhood boys, they left marks and stung.

One time the tree became a mortuary, with its own private cemetery nearby, where we took our dead Easter chick. The vehicle was a white toy ambulance, which had a back door that opened onto a flat floor. With tears in our eyes, Julieta and I placed our dead chick in a match box, which served as a coffin. We lived across the street from Brings Funeral Home and a block from the Tucson Mortuary, so funerals were a natural part of life, but death was still sad. Later when some boys dug up our coffin, sadness turned to anger. We finally got our chick back and reburied it secretly, in an unmarked grave, near mi arbol.

Mi arbol was also a nice place to read, since it was kitty-cornered from the main library. Most often, mi arbol was a home, with both an upstairs and a downstairs. Rooms were fashioned by tying the limbs, this way one time and another way another time. The tree limbs bent and never complained. In spring time, the tree became a flower shop with a profusion of lilac-like flowers, full of a sweet aroma. It was then that we girls claimed the tree. These flowers were fashioned into hats and leis and pinned everywhere. But after the flowers dried out and the berries were left, the boys took possession, especially when the berries became hard, dark, tiny missiles.

After we moved away, I would stop by the tree and visit once in a while and remember all the good times. One year the tree looked devasted, almost dry, with broken limbs. For a while I drove over and watered it, but that became too difficult, so I stopped. I felt sad and stopped going by altogether. To my surprise, when I finally got back to it, the tree looked healthier and happier than ever. It was stronger, greener and rested. Mi arbol is located north of the newly restored Temple of Music and Art. It now peeks over a recently constructed wall on South Scott Avenue. This tree is a part of my life, and, with all the things going on around that block, I am so glad this tree survived. It never gave up. It is still there, and I love mi arbol. *Hasta la vista.*

# Mexican Traditions for All Souls Day Remember Dead

In two weeks, we will soon celebrate Halloween in the United States. A few days later, in Mexico, people will celebrate *El Dia de los Muertos*, the Day of the Dead, on All Souls Day, Friday, November 2.

The meaning of death takes on a different feeling in many Mexican families, especially on that day. Unlike Halloween, All Souls Day is not a day of ghouls, but one of remembering those who have died. It is a day of visiting and celebrating between the dead and the living. Altars are set up in homes with *ofrendas* (offerings) to the dead, including their favorite foods, breads, pastries, candy and toys. Photographs of the dead are prominently displayed.

In preparation for the event, graves and graveyards are spruced up for the celebrations that will be held there. During the celebrations, candles and incense are lit at the graves. Flowers are placed there. Food and beverages are consumed while music is played and *pláticas* (talks with the departed), the guests of honor, are held.

Only at this time of year is *Pan de los Muertos* (Bread of the Dead) baked, and specially decorated for this celebration. Sugar-skull candy magically appear in the bakeries. Names are prominently displayed across their foreheads in bright colors, with painted flowers. All remind us of the existence of life in death. All types of different flowers—fresh, silk, plastic, tin, foam and clay— are fashioned into the circular shape of wreaths of eternity or in the shape of the cross of resurrection, promising reunion with all our loved ones.

Years ago, in the Old Pueblo, *velorios* (wakes) were held at home and occasionally still are. In small Mexican towns, this custom is still followed. In Tucson, we Mexican Americans now most often refer to these as *rosarios*. These velorios are all-night vigils, with rosaries and prayers to accompany the dead soul on its journey to the next stage of existence. Usually menudo and coffee or alcoholic drinks, to fortify the body and soul, are served to guests by the grieving family. Of course, guests also bring food to share.

In the morning, the body is accompanied to the church for its final religious service and then the procession, often with music, is taken to its earthly resting place. The grave is dug by friends and family, as it is still sometimes done in Tucson and surrounding areas. It is a final tribute and wonderful experience that helps to work out deep feelings of sorrow This is followed by the family and friends again joining the surviving family members to share a meal, comfort the sorrowing, and remember the departed.

The following day the *novenario* begins. This is the praying of the rosary for nine consecutive nights. The modern version is a one day, nine-hour novenario. *Nueve* (nine), was originally chosen because of the nine-day journey Mary and Joseph traditionally took to Bethlehem.

At the most recent rosario I attended, I saw a young, handsome, dark-skinned boy approach the pale blue-satin lined open coffin. I was at the kneeler, praying the 23rd Psalm. He slowly, deliberately reached with one hand into the coffin and lightly touched the clasped hands of the corpse, in which two rosaries were intertwined. The head was veiled in a small black lace head covering. Its scalloped edge framed her calm, peaceful face. The young man looked at her lovingly. As he turned to face her, he stretched the index and middle fingers of his right hand and ever so gently and tenderly stroked her forehead a number of times in a downward motion to the furrows of her brow. Finally, he followed the contour of her bridge with his finger tips and then down her finely shaped nose. He continued to do this as he looked into her sleeping face.

Then he looked towards me. His eyes looked sadly resigned, but not desolate. "Was she your grandmother, *tu abuelita*?" I asked. He seemed not to understand but said in a quiet voice. "*Es mi nana, todavia*" (She is still my abuelita).

And so, she is, dead or alive. She is still his grandmother, spiritually. Even those who have died have the power of the spirit, the power of love that brings family and friends to console and to celebrate life and death, at velorios and on *El Dia de los Muertos. Hasta la vista.*

# Fred Acosta Devotes Life to Helping Youth

Since we are approaching Thanksgiving, which focuses on being thankful, I chose to write about a man and his kids who personify this virtue.

Fred Acosta is the director of the Tucson Job Corps. This is a government job training program for 16- to 23-year-olds. Of all the people I know, Acosta refers constantly to and is thankful for his teachers, his mentors, as he calls them. They cared enough about him to give of themselves to him. Now, in turn, Acosta gives of himself to his kids at the Tucson Job Corps.

Acosta recalled:

> I was born in a little town, Deming, in southern New Mexico, in my grand-mother's house. I can actually go to that house today and see the spot where I came into the world. My grandmother was Carmen Pereda Giron Chavez and she had a tremendous influence on me. She did not read or write nor speak English. She spoke Spanish. But she did not read or write it, either, and still the priest would come and ask her about canon law.

By 1943, when his family moved to Tucson, Acosta was already "the class clown." Unfortunately, at a tender age, a schoolteacher had humiliated him in front of his classmates and as a result Acosta shut down academically. "I didn't know my numbers, I didn't know my letters, I didn't know anything, I just survived." He continued:

> One day as I was walking on the school ground, a teacher asked me, 'You going to college?' I just strutted away. He kicked me and I fell, but I wasn't about to cry. The next day as I walked by, he repeated the question and immediately I answered, 'Yes, sir.' He was my math teacher, Raymond Felix, and he became

my first mentor. He tutored me every school day and he convinced Maggie Ybarra to tutor me in language arts and in geography, every single day. After a while, I quit clowning. What would have happened to me if that man had not been there? At Safford Junior High, Mr. Leslie Cronk was my homeroom teacher, a good algebra instructor, and my mentor there.

At Tucson High, I had more mentors, Hank Egbert and Elbert Brooks, both positive and strong. When I was feeling down, Miss Eva Royce would ask me, 'How are you doing, Frederick?' If there was someone who really helped me, it was Francis Smith, my counselor. I had a good sophomore year. Baseball was my favorite sport and Red Greer, head coach, was a good man, and Lowell Bailey was another good man. Someone real positive was my wrestling coach, Ken Pearson. Doc J.A. Van Horne taught physics and he was also a good track coach. They were all my mentors.

After graduation, Acosta worked at Southern Pacific Railroad as a boilermaker and also attended the University of Arizona. In 1953, he joined the Marines, and in 1954 married Norma Manciet. Then, he was stationed in Korea, along with a few other Tucsonans. Acosta said:

I want my students to know that he or she is special. We are all unique. What made our country great was our public education That is what I try to do here. We try to create an environment of dignity, of self-esteem and get these kids back into the system. I tell them, this place is about life. Who are you? Where do you come from? You are unique. We all are. Many kids let things happen to them. We give them role models. We know they have histories of making poor decisions. I tell them, 'You have to learn to make good decisions.' This place is oriented to the kids. I have a gang going here. A good gang and it is my gang. I want them to live good lives. I have respect and affection for these kids and that is what life is really about.

*Hasta la vista.*

1991

# The Baking of *Rosca* is a Special Tradition

Happy New Year *y Próspero Año Nuevo*!

This Sunday is the day the children put out their shoes in some places and also the day of receiving the gifts. It is also known in Mexico and among Mexican American families, *as El Dia de los Santos Reyes* and *El Dia de la Rosca*. The rosca is a special bread that is baked exclusively to be served, shared and eaten on this day. It is formed into a circle or oval and in it is placed one, two, three or four tiny dolls. They are not visible from the outside of the ring. But they are there.

Those carrying on this tradition hold an open house. Family and friends call on each other. At each home, all partake of a slice of the rosca. Now one or more persons will have the little, tiny doll representing Baby Jesus, in their slice of rosca. That lucky person takes the Baby Jesus from the Nacimiento of the hosts' home. That person "dresses" the baby in beautiful white satin, sateen, velvet or lace with gold trim, and makes a suitable pillow for the baby to lie upon. This they will then place on a tray and surround with goodies such as chocolates, nuts and caramels.

On February 2, which is called *El Dia de la Candelaria*, they will present the "baby" back to the hosts. A celebration follows. This gesture gets the guests involved with the hosts. They now enlarge their family spiritually by the ritual of being co-parents to the baby Jesus. The "baby" is often taken to church on that day and blessed by the priest. Often *compadres* attend mass together prior to the celebration. Sometimes the mass can be said at the home, where the celebration will take place.

On January, 6, the ritual is festive but low-key. On the day of the return, the celebration is big. It can be humble or fancy, but big in that the day is full of emotional and spiritual blessings. Often *bonos* are given, which means the *padrinos* (godparents) give out coins to the poor, particularly the children and also to the guests. Often small gifts are exchanged between the *compadres* as remembrances.

Last year I became a comadre to Jesusita and Arturo Robles in this manner. Lujan's Bakery is baking special roscas the public can buy. This year they sent their consultant, Luis de la Torre, to Mexico to purchase the glazed fruit used in the rosca. Other Mexican bakeries might also have them. It is a fine tradition. In 1960 while visiting our cousins, the Zayas family in Guadalajara, my husband and I found a "baby" in each of our slices and subsequently had a party, here in Tucson, to which we invited everybody. May you be blessed with a lot of new compadres and comadres this New Year. May you have a healthy, joyous, beautiful 1991—full of truth, light and peace. *Cariñosamente y hasta la vista*, Alva.

# Gulf Crisis Evokes Memories of 1941

This past week I was in New Orleans, attending a conference for the 25th anniversary of Title V. Title V is part of the Older Americans Act, which provides job training to Americans who are 55 years of age or older and whose income level qualifies them for the program.

On the last night of the conference more than 1,000 people attended a big banquet. It was in the Grand Ballroom at the Sheraton, and the entire room was decorated in silver and blue shining, glittering and dazzling pre-Mardi Gras decor. The music was jazz, New Orleans style, and when they played the familiar song, "When the Saints Come Marching In," one of the guests remarked, "This will probably be the last big celebration all of us will attend before the Persian Gulf War begins." It was a gripping moment for all of us.

My mind immediately recalled December 7, 1941, in downtown Tucson. At lunchtime that day, my family was at Tom's Cafe, on Ninth Street across from the Coronado Hotel where The Shanty now stands. That's where we first heard some rumors about the Japanese bombing some place. It was so vague that my father and mother did not even discuss it. As our Sunday treat, our parents either went with us or dropped my little sister, Julietita, and me off at the Fox Theater on Congress Street. That day they did not go. As my sister and I walked in the theater, we spotted neighborhood kids, the Valencias, and sat with them. About halfway through the first movie, suddenly the screen went dark, along with the rest of the theater. Then the white spotlight came on, illuminating the manager as he walked across the stage. He made an announcement, "All military personnel are to report to the local Air Force base immediately. This morning the Japanese military air forces bombed Pearl Harbor. Report immediately." As soon as he made this announcement, we could see young men get up and leave the theater.

One of the neighbors, turned to Julietita and me and said, "You know what this means, don't you? Your father will be taken to Pearl Harbor and he will be killed." I got a lump in my throat and began crying. Julietita, always calm, said, "Alvita, don't pay attention to her. She does not know anything." We stayed and watched the rest of the show. By the time we left it was dark. Once home, we ran upstairs and heard Mother and Father listening to the news on the old Philco radio. They told us that everything was going to be all right. On Monday morning, December 8, the principal of Safford Elementary School, Alice Fomer (Dunam), had all of the school children, grades one through six, taken into the few rooms where radios were available so that we all could hear President Franklin Delano Roosevelt declare war.

This weekend, I listened to all our men and women in Congress, who appear to be sincerely interested in representing their constituents. And I have read as much as possible. Like others, I am trying to understand both sides. On Sunday morning, at my parents' house, we talked about the Persian Gulf situation, and then I spent part of the afternoon visiting friends. Even though we were watching the football games, everywhere the conversation included or focused on the imminent war.

It is certain that we cannot see the many ramifications that will touch all of us now, and future generations, by our actions. Opinions range from "It will be over in two days" to "This is the beginning of the third world war." Most of us have neither the background, the training, the facts nor the wisdom to know who or what is best. Only time will tell. All we can hope for is that all negative aspects are kept to a minimum and all we can do is pray for God to guide us. *Hasta la vista.*

# Sister-in-law's Death Evokes Fond Memories

My sister-in-law, Margaret Torres Donsky, died recently. Sad as that was getting together with family and friends who had not seen each other for some time was so pleasant. We talked about many different things, old and new. We shared lots of photographs. Some were taken at La Nopalera Photography Studio.

Margaret was born here in Tucson and lived here almost all her life. She graduated from Tucson High School and went on to work for Bendy Gross, developing photographs. They developed negatives for many drugstores. Before World War Il she went to work for Virginia Manzo, owner of the La Nopalera Photography Studio. It was located immediately south of the downtown Fox Theater on West Congress Street.

Every Mexican American in the Old Pueblo knew the place. Manzo always had photographs on display inside and outside the studio. Almost everyone who went to the Fox would stop outside La Nopalera to see who had been married the month before. We would see

La Nopalera Studio
**WELCOMES**
**The First Baby**
of
**The New Year**

**Our Prize An 8x10 Picture**

Due to the acute film shortage, which means our allotments of films are much smaller, we are unable to take as many baby pictures as in previous years. . . . But we will do our best to accommodate as many of our patrons as possible.

**La Nopalera Studios**

21 W. Congress                Virginia K. Manzo

FIGURE 8.1  Advertisement that references WWII shortages. *Citizen*, December 31, 1943, p.6.

not only the bride and groom but often the entire wedding party. Eventually, we saw the couple's first baby, in a photograph. At First Communion time, the windows were full of little girls pictured in their lovely veils, white dresses and religious artifacts. The little boys naturally reflected the same settings in their suits. Later we saw the boys in uniforms serving their country.

Virginia Manzo, the owner, was also the photographer. Vickie Martinez was the developer and Margaret [sister-in-law] was the touch-up person. She also did any coloration necessary, because the photographs were in black and white or brown and white. Margaret was married Stan Donsky in 1958, and like most of us in those days, she became a homemaker. Margaret was a good neighbor, a good friend and to me always a good sister. Many of us will miss her. *Hasta la vista. Cariñosamente, Alva.*

# Tucson Street Names Took Interesting Turns

By now everyone probably has heard that the famous rodeo parade will not be going through downtown Tucson. For natives such as me, it is difficult to get excited about the new turn it is taking. At the same time, we know that life is constantly changing and we hope that this new route turns out to be a good one.

It is doubtful that my great grandfather, Onofre Navarro, who already was in this area when John B. Mills Jr. drew the first map of Tucson in 1862, could even have dreamed that Tucson would someday get to be as large and populated as it is today. But then the Indians who lived here in their pit houses in what is now downtown Tucson between 700 and 900 never saw what Onofre saw, either.

As you can see in the map, the only words in English were, "Map of Tucson, surveyed by order of. . . ." All of the street names still appear in Spanish. Tucson itself was named by the native Indians, and they called it in their native tongue, either "Spring at the foot of the mountain" or "Spring at the foot of the black mountain." The mountain they referred to was Sentinel Peak, commonly called "A" Mountain. Calle Real was in reality part of the Camino Real, which was the King's (of Spain) Highway and which came from Mexico. Tucson did not become part of the United States of America until the Gadsden Purchase was signed in Mesilla, New Mexico, in Santa Ana County, of which Tucson was then a part. Mesilla was the county seat. It was ratified and took effect in 1854 but for several years Mexican troops remained here.

There is a legend that when the people found out that Mexico had sold the area they became angry, took some legal documents, built a fire in the area shown on the map as Plaza de la Mesilla and burned the papers in protest to the Mexican government.

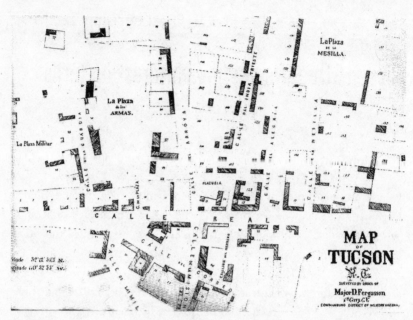

FIGURE 8.2 The 1862 map of Tucson by David Fergusson.

Calle de la Mesilla remained until urban renewal in the '60s, and then the little part that was left was renamed Calle Arruza [after bullfighter Carlos Arruza]. It would have been nice to have kept the original name, which went back so far, especially since we have nothing to do with bullfights here. The street shown as Calle del Alegria means "Street of Happiness." It ran parallel to Calle del India Trieste, which in correct Spanish should read either Calle de la India (female) Triste, or Calle del Indio (male) Triste. The first one means "Street of the Sad Indian Woman"; the second one means "Street of the Sad Indian Man." But either way it conveyed sadness.

The street shown as Calle del Arroyo is now Pennington Street, and it bordered the old Presidio wall. Adobe bricks for the wall were made from the mud in that area and so it became more and more of an arroyo or stream. Calle de la Guadia is now Alameda and was inside the Presidio, where the soldiers had their barracks.

Calle de las Milpas led to the fields, which each family was allotted in order to grow its vegetables. Calle del Correo led to the Post Office and Calle de la Mision, of course, led to San Xavier Mission. Later Calle Real became

Main Street, Happiness and Sad Indian became Congress Street and Campo which later became Camp and still later Broadway.

Some changes can turn out to be good. I would like to see Calle Real resurrected in some way; after all, it was the street the Spaniards took on their way to found San Francisco in 1776. We need to know about the old times and the old-timers and where they went and where we are going. *Hasta la vista.*

# Meyer Street Cleaner Regrets Urban Renewal

Roberto Garcia is a hometown boy. Actually, he is a 72-year-old youthful person who has survived Tucson's growing up. What do I mean by that? Let me tell you just a bit about him.

His father, Margarito Garcia, was born in Hermosillo, Sonora and became a tailor. His mother, Maria Guadalupe Rubalcava, was born in Tucson. His father came to Tucson during the Mexican Revolution. Roberto relates that:

> My dad had a tailor shop located at 72 South Meyer called Garden City Tailor. He chose that name because he ordered suiting material from a company of the same name. To complement his shop, Dad added a little dry-cleaning service.
>
> My brother Henry and I started working there when we were little boys. By the time we were 12 and 14, we knew pretty much about the business. When I was 16, I convinced my dad to charge 25 cents to clean a pair of pants and to expand the dry-cleaning service. I remember that one Christmas we made a whole $160. The old man thought he was rich. It was a lot of money then. During the Depression we moved to 166 South Meyer.
>
> I met my wife, Sarah Benitez, also a native Tucsonan, in 1939 working for Wallace Cleaners. She was a silk finisher. During WWII, I joined the Marines and served with the South Pacific fleet. The only ambition I had was to come back to Meyer Street and press pants. But going into the service was my best education because that taught me I wasn't so dumb, and that was when I decided that I was going to get the pay that I was worth and I wanted to be the Captain.
>
> In 1947, Sarah and I were married, and right from the beginning she helped me at work. By the time Dad died at age 61, Henry and I already owned the business. I never missed a day's work. I had vitality, energy and nerve. The

reason I mention this is because when urban renewal came around and city officials wanted was to get us out, not help us renew. To this day I feel I was underpaid for my building and all the equipment we had acquired over the years. At the same time, my customers were being moved out until the area became depopulated, but I was looking ahead.

In 1969 Henry sold out his part of the business to me. Meanwhile, I was running a survey trying to decide where to locate my new Garcia's Cleaners. It was not by chance that we ended up at this location on the corner of South Fifth and East 22nd. I did a lot of calculating. We had to build everything and buy new equipment and move things smoothly. I still feel rage when I recall urban renewal.

I don't have to worry about too much anymore. I'm in no need. I'm not rich but I'm comfortable knowing that my children are going on to better things and I will continue working. I like working, within reason. We meet people we would never have met if we had retired and stayed home. We have *muchos* old-timers from the days on Meyer Street who still bring their dry cleaning here.

There have been many changes in this business because of the new materials, and for a while rayon and silks and linens disappeared, but like the good old days they came back. Actually, people can get along without these services. It depends on the standard of your appearance.

Both Garcias say they like the old days. Sarah Garcia says, "I thought Tucson was beautiful." Roberto Garcia agrees, saying, "So was Meyer Street where I was born, raised and did business. It was my playground, and everybody knew everybody."

I have always been in awe of those businessmen and women who survived urban renewal. In the midst of change, the Old Pueblo continues. *Hasta la vista.*

# Wedding Merges Cultures, Traditions

I recently attended a most interesting wedding. It was held at a Presbyterian church, uniting an Anglo and a Mexican American. This wedding not only united two people from different ethnic backgrounds, but it did so with an interdenominational feeling.

Along with the very beautiful and sacred wedding vows, the traditional Mexican ritual of using a *padrino* and a *madrina de laso* (man and maid of honor of the rosary) with the large double ring of simulated pearls representing a rosary were part of the service. It also had a wonderful mixture of songs that included the favorite "Ave Maria." It was very nice to see that unity instead of division is thriving in our Tucson religious community.

\* \* \*

This year the Ballet Folklórico Mexicana de Angel Hernandez gave a most enjoyable performance on June 1 at the University of Arizona's Centennial Hall. Executive director Mercedes Guerrero, with the help of visiting director Jose Luis Cardenas Quirarte of Guadalajara, gave us an enchanting evening.

The late Angel Hernandez was a native of Guadalajara, Jalisco, Mexico. In 1971 he was employed by Pima Community College to teach Mexican *bailes folklóricos* and *artes populares* from Mexico. He founded the Grupo Folklórico de Pima College, the Instituto de Folklore Mexicano and the Ballet Folklórico Mexica. Most of our present folklórico dancing groups emerged from these beginnings, and I feel that Tucson should have a worthy memorial to him at some future time because of the excellent artistic training he brought as an example of his own beliefs and teachings.

\* \* \*

Also, I'd like to take this opportunity to thank all of you faithful and dear readers who correspond with me. I will eventually get in touch with each of you or try to get the information you request. *Hasta la vista.*

# Nani, Like the Old Pueblo, More Beautiful Every Year

Happy Birthday, Nani. Therecita Torres, my mother-in-law, says she isn't counting birthdays anymore, just celebrating them.

A fun way to commemorate a birthday is compare the olden days with today. So, I went to the library and looked up October 5, 1898, to see what was happening in the Old Pueblo on the day Nani was born. I am sharing that with you readers, just for the fun of it. "Tucson the Healers Mecca and Capital's Opportunity," said a headline in the *Arizona Daily Star*. The column continued:

> The climate is dry and pleasant during the entire year. During the months of June, July and August, average temperature is about 90 degrees but there is a little humidity in the atmosphere. While three of the summer months are warm during the day, the nights are always cool. This is on account of the rarified conditions of the atmosphere which becomes instantly cool on the setting of the sun. The fall, winter and spring months can be compared with the Italian clime. There is little or no frost. Flowers bloom during the entire winter months and much of the shrubbery retains its foliage. As compared with Southern California, Tucson and the surrounding area is far superior in every respect.

The same newspaper ran an advertisement from Hotel Redondo in Redondo Beach, Calif., which tells the readers to: "Avoid the heat of September and arrange your Vacation here." It calls the hotel "Arizona's favorite Seaside Resort."

It would be interesting to know if our weather has changed that much since then. If so, that might explain why people could live here without coolers and refrigeration back then. Another paragraph goes on about Tucson industries. "Tucson has a population of 10,000, about one-third Mexican descent. It is the commercial center for Southwestern Arizona and Northern Sonora, Mexico. It is the seat of Pima County. The location of the U.S. Surveyor General Office and the U.S. Land Office, the U.S. District Court and the U.S. Marshalls office." It does not mention how many are employed in these industries or any other, but we assume that all able-bodied men were gainfully employed, as there was no way to survive otherwise.

The article continues, "It is the headquarters of two divisions of the Southern Pacific Railroad comprising over 600 miles of line, also shops, roundhouses, etc. The monthly [company] payroll averages from $60, 000 to $70,000 to the employees which add vitality to the commercial prosperity of the city." We know Tucson was a progressive city because we also learn that, "The city is lighted with electricity and gas and telephone, and street roadways are well maintained. The water is supplied from the Santa Cruz River and is absolutely pure."

The most frequent, well-placed and large advertisements were for hotels. It appears we had nine of them, a score of restaurants and several lodging houses. The cost of lodging at the hotels ranged from $1.50 to $5 per day, but if you stayed by the month it ranged from $5 to $15. The Hall, a family hotel advertised first-class service. The Hotel San Augustine (which was one of the uses of the old San Agustín Church on the Plaza de la Mesilla after the new Cathedral was built) let us know it had all the modern conveniences of a first-class hotel, and the New Orndorff Hotel told us "Everything is First Class." So, then as now, we had a lot of classy hotels here.

Among our restaurants we had a French one with meals offered at all hours, and we had a big advertisement from a Mrs. M. Lewis, who not only offered hairdressing and manicures, but body and facial massages, as well as vapor baths at ladies' homes and a treatment to prevent hair from falling out.

We also had an Opera Bath house, and Eagle Mills produced "Gold Dust Flour." We had doctors and lawyers, banks, bicycle shops and livery stables. There was also an ad for Dr. Pierce's Pleasant Pellets for constipation and biliousness (bad digestion).

I suppose this paper was mailed all over the U.S. because some of the news included the location of Tucson, 500 miles east of Los Angeles, 300 miles north of El Paso and 670 miles south of Denver. At least we knew where we were.

Anyway, Nani is sure healthy. She takes care of herself, takes walks every day, has no problem hearing, and can see fairly well. She has a fantastic appetite, is of a calm, sweet nature. She grows lovelier each year, just like our Old Pueblo. *Hasta la vista.*

# Club Duette Members' Business is Friendship

I was just 15 years young [1947] when I was invited to join Club Mavis, a new girl's social club of Mexican American native *Tucsonenses*.

At that time members met on a weekly basis at their respective homes. Good food made by our *mamacitas* was served, accompanied by giggles and laughter, with just a little bit of business conducted. It consisted of planning fun events, particularly *bailes*, dances. Eventually, our bailes began making a profit, especially our New Year's Eve Dance, always held at El Casino Ballroom. We also had an annual midsummer *Baile de Cascarones*. We had everyone save clean, empty eggshells. Then for many meetings we made well over a thousand pretty, colorful, confetti-filled cascarones. The highlight of the dance was when cascarones were cracked on people's heads. We used the profits to purchase shoes and glasses for students who could not afford them. Our other events, picnics and luncheons for our mothers, made no money.

Then we began to have wedding showers and more wedding showers, until one year we had 12. When a member was wed, she had to leave the club, and a new member came in. By then the "old married women" decided to regroup and chose the name Club Duette. We included our spouses for a while, but that turned out to be a disaster. All they wanted to do was play cards into the wee hours. We also needed more food and beverages. It got too expensive and difficult. So, at one meeting, the women went into an adjoining room, voted all the men out, set a different meeting date and never included spouses again. Even so, they always helped us decorate and lug equipment to our *puestos* (booths) when we participated in typical Tucson fiestas.

In addition to helping others, we also helped each other every way possible, and in the case of death, we gave immediate financial help to the surviving spouse. When one couple suddenly became parents to two babies, instead of one, we doubled necessary items. We have had a lot of baby showers and shared a lot of advice on how to handle life's problems.

When we first regrouped as Club Duette, we continued with the old rules from Club Mavis, such as dropping members who miss three consecutive meetings. But we are past that now because we have become true friends. We have what we call Sunshine Callers, who call the rest of us when there is a necessity, such as a health challenge, or to remind us of happy events, anniversaries, births or weddings. Meeting with the girls three weeks after my dear husband, Alberto died in 1976, was of great help to me in the healing process. Their unconditional support in listening to me and visiting and including me in their lives was immeasurably helpful. At our last meeting, we all sat around my dining room table and talked about the death of parents and how to cope with it.

Members have recently lost parents. One member let us know that our meetings and concern about her at this sad time made her great sadness more bearable. This conversation was precious, thoughtful and so important that our meeting was convened almost two hours later than usual. But our business is friendship more than anything else. Over the years we greet each other with *besitos y abrazos*, hugs and kisses, and part the same way. Two of our members have died, and we keep their dear memories alive in our reminiscing. We celebrate that we knew them.

Club Mavis no longer exists, but Club Duette is still going strong. We still have social events and we help particular families who need help, but most of all we have wonderful friendships because we grew to have a better understanding of what is important in life, more compassion for others, and most of all lots and lots and lots of love. Club Duette is a blessing to me. *Hasta la vista.*

1992

# A Child's Memory of Entrepreneurship

Making money when you are a child is not easy, but when you are trying to buy gifts for your family and friends, it becomes important, so you need to be creative. One of our most lucrative business enterprises, when Julietita and I were very young [1939], was selling cookies. Our business could have rivaled the Girl Scouts' cookie sales.

At a certain time in our young lives, our mother went to work as a seamstress for Jacome's department store, then located on Congress Street. We lived a few blocks from there, on Scott Avenue and McCormick Street, next to the Temple of Music and Art. The end of McCormick Street intersected Stone Avenue, about one short block south of St. Augustine Cathedral. It was a pretty busy street for foot traffic, because it was near the church and also a main street to get downtown from the southern part of the city.

Selling something people would want to buy at a reasonable price gave us a serious research challenge. The product could not cost us anything, since we had no capital. It had to be something in supply and it had to be something we could manage by ourselves. First, we thought of lemonade. We always had sugar at home, and usually lemons. But our ice supply was dismal—two little trays in a small freezing compartment. Then we would have to provide glasses, which we would have to carry back and forth to wash and dry, and which might break. In addition, there was some labor involved in making and lugging the beverage to the corner on Stone Avenue. Our research had found the perfect location, but our product was as yet unchosen. Ice cream would be wonderful but impossible. Cake would be nice but not available in the quantities needed on a daily basis. What was possible and yummy and in constant supply were Mama's homemade cookies. We had found the perfect product.

FIGURE 9.1 Alva and Julieta in 1945. Courtesy Alva B. Torres.

First, I fashioned a tray, complete with ribbons, to place around Julieti-ta's neck, much like the cigarette trays we often saw in the movies in those days. Julietita was chosen as the salesgirl, as I thought her age, then 4, and her looks, better than mine. I was 7. Anyway, she could hold the box and I would take care of the cashiering, as I was older and could make change. I could also run home as soon as our supply ran low to wrap more cookies in wax paper, four to a package. These would sell for a nickel a package. We had a variety of cookies to offer: chocolate chip, peanut butter, oatmeal or sometimes pinwheels filled with dates, and once in a while something else Mama was just trying out.

We did fantastic business. Our profit was mounting and we had no overhead. But one day the star saleslady, Julietita, refused to sell anymore. She said the sun was getting too hot and she was having a hard time standing in the shadows of the light post all the time. She was getting bored, and besides, we had made a lot of money by now. On top of everything else, she said she wanted to eat cookies again. All this time we had had to give up eating the delicious cookies, as we were selling so many. Mama had begun to comment on the amount of *galletitas* (cookies) we and our friends were eating.

Although we wanted to surprise her and Papá and each other with Christmas gifts, we closed down. The happiest was Julietita. I had regrets. We had given up our big chance. One consolation was that I could now eat cookies with my milk, instead of soda crackers with jelly. Anyway, I knew that someday we would go into business again, as sure as we would need money. We would just have to find something else to sell, with no overhead. Eventually we did. That's *otro cuento*, another story.

Mother never did find out until years later when friends asked her if we were doing better. Others had made comments such as, "You and Miguel must be in better circumstances. *No hemos visto a las niñas ultimamente en la esquina* (We haven't seen the children lately at the corner)." She did not know what they were talking about. We never told her until we grew up. By then all she could do was laugh. If any of our cookie customers are still around, *muchas gracias. Hasta la vista.*

# CARA an Exhibit Worthwhile to See

"CARA: Chicano Art Resistance and Affirmation," on exhibit at the Tucson Museum of Art, 140 North Main Avenue, will close April 5, less than a month from now. If you have not yet seen it, I urge you to do so. It is a thought-provoking exhibition and an important component of the Festival Chicano Del Tucson.

In conjunction with the exhibit, a symposium, "CARAS: The Many Faces of the Chicano Community," was held last month. Debra Padilla, managing director of the Borderlands Theater, coordinated the symposium, so I paid her a visit and asked how she got involved. She said:

> The starting ground was when I went to Los Angeles to see CARA. I was really inspired. I found out it was coming to Tucson and I wanted to know what I could do to assist in all of the ancillary programming. I spoke to Barclay Goldsmith, Raquel Goldsmith and Lupe Castillo, all leaders in our community. Lupe thought that we could commission Sylvia Woods, a playwright and educator, to write a play. I also contacted the Arizona Center for the Media Arts and suggested a Chicano film series. And I spoke with members of Arte Hispano and Dinnerware, both local art groups, and asked them how they wanted to participate. All of them became interested in being part of the festival. I wanted another vehicle or venue, of a moment in time, when we could all be in a situation where our minds were being filled with history, political, cultural and educational ramification of the *movimiento*—Chicano civil rights movement. So, I thought of the symposium. I put together the proposal and went to Bob Yasin, executive director of Tucson Museum of Art, and told him, 'As an ethnic arts group, here is what we can do for you in relation to the whole show.' He was very pleased. The festival has been in the planning for over a year.

Events held in conjunction with the CARA exhibition:

● Opening reception, noon-4 p.m. Jan. 19, free and open to the public at Tucson Museum of Art, 140 N. Main Ave.

● "CARAS: The Many Faces of the Chicano/A Community," described as "a humanist symposium," Feb. 7 and 8 in the Leo Rich Theater at the Tucson Convention Center, from 9:30 a.m.-5:30 p.m. each day, with a reception at TMA from 6-8 p.m. following the Saturday presentations. Keynote speaker is Tomas Ybarra Frausto of the Rockefeller Foundation and also a major participant in the Chicano movement and a primary interpreter of its literary and artistic history.

● Festival Chicano del Tucson is a broad-based cultural accompaniment to the exhibition. In addition to the CARA exhibition, "Counter Colon-ialismo," a show of artworks that present alternative views of history and aesthetics will be presented at Dinnerware Artists' Cooperative Gallery, 135 E. Congress St., and at Pima Community College Fine Arts Complex, 2202 W. Anklam Road, from Jan. 28-March 2.

● Cine Chicano Film Series, presented by the Arizona Center for the Media Arts, will run Jan. 30-March 15 at the Screening Room, 127 E. Congress St. Times are: Thursdays at 7:30 p.m. and Sundays at 3 and 7:30 p.m. Admission is $3. Call 628-1737 for programming information.

● "Latins Anonymous," an irreverent comedy presented by Borderlands Theater, will have performances March 12-15, 19, 20, 21, 22. Times are 8 p.m. Thursday, Friday and Saturday and 3 p.m. Sunday at the Pima College Center for the Arts, Proscenium Theatre. Tickets are $10 general admission or $8 for senior citizens and students. For more information, call 882-8607. A staged reading of a play by Sylviana Wood will be held. Time and place to be announced.

● A music festival, "Viva Tucson," presented by Chicanos por la Causa on March 19, 20, 21. Time and place to be announced.

● "Teatro Campesino," presented by Teatro Carmen, will be held March 25 and 26. Time and place to be announced.

FIGURE 9.2  Advertisement for CARA events. *Citizen*, January, 16, 1992, p.10.

For those of you who were unable to attend, Tomás Ybarra-Frausto, assistant director of arts from the Rockefeller Foundation, was the keynote speaker. He spoke of being held in place by global networks of power. He spoke of the Chicano art movement, which rose parallel to the political movement. He also spoke of ideas that move from L.A. to Mexico, from Bolivia to Barcelona and back to the barrios. Padilla concluded, "This whole experience speaks favorably of the power of partnerships and collaborations."

Another part of the festival is Borderland Theater's production of Latins Anonymous. It played in Tucson last year and received wonderful reviews. It will be presented from Thursday through March 22 in the Pima Community College Center for the Arts, Proscenium Theatre. Performance times will be 8 p.m. Thursdays through Saturdays and 3 p.m. Sundays. I saw it last time and plan to see it again. It is hilarious, witty and entertaining. For more information or tickets call 882–8607.

For information on "CARA: Chicano Art, Resistance and Affirmation," call the Tucson Museum of Art, 624–2333. The museum is open seven days a week during the exhibition, and whether you like the show or not, it at least gives us all another view of America. *Hasta la vista.*

# Carrillo School Praised for Teaching

On March 24, many former students and friends of Carrillo Intermediate Magnet School, at 440 South Main Avenue, enjoyed a ceremony marking this historic place of learning with bilingual site markers placed by the Tucson-Pima County Historical Commission. Among the speakers, Councilwoman Molly McKasson addressed the audience in both languages, reinforcing the self-esteem of the neighborhood children who attend this A-plus school, which means it ranks high in the state because of the quality of education and the parent involvement.

Carmen Camacho, the community representative who helped coordinate the ceremony, explained that the school has a Carrillo Excellence Honors Program, which means students can work on a contract and receive special academic education by working on extra math, computer, or fine arts and drama projects. This is in addition to their regular work. It was just such a classroom project that first worked on an original cookbook in 1980. Out of this came an updated *Tucson Festival of Foods.** It is dedicated to the future students and parents of Carrillo School and the people of Barrio Viejo, (Old Neighborhood). Some of the former students include Ralph Martinez and Patricia Flores. Their father, Rafael B. Martinez, was Carrillo's first custodian, in 1930. Gilbert Araneta, another former student, fondly remembers his guitar. "Me acuerdo de su guitarra," said Araneta. Others in attendance were the Martinez "girls," Henrietta Martinez De Meester and Isola Jacobs Martinez. Her son Gilbert Martinez was also there, as was Hector Garcia, who has

---

*Over the years, Carrillo School students have produced a number of publications: *Tales Told in Our Barrio* (1984), *Tucson Festival of Foods* (1985), *Our Hispanic Role Models* (1988), *Celebrations in Our Pueblo* (1985), and *Architecture in Our Barrio* (2003). All are available at Special Collections at the University of Arizona Library.

enough memories to write a book himself. He stood in line to sign the guest
book with Alfred Carley and Art Carrillo Strong. We do not know who the
oldest guest was, as no one admitted to that, but we know the youngest was
6 weeks young—Taylor de la Garza, great great-great grandson of Leopoldo
Carrillo, for whom the school is named.

Along with the cookbook, the school has published three other books,
all available at the school. One, *Tales Told in Our Barrio*, edited by Carol
Cribbet Bell, librarian, quotes Isabel Urias, who still resides in the neighborhood as saying, "Sometimes on the playground of Carrillo School there
appear apparitions of the lake that used to be here." This refers to the lake
that was part of Elysian Gardens, belonging to Leopoldo. These books are
used not only for a layman's historical reference, but, just as important, as
a way for children to express the essence of a barrio as it applies to those of
Mexican Heritage, and thus help bridge the gaps which exist in our own Old
Pueblo. *Hasta la vista.*

# Easter is a Time for Family and Memories

This Easter Sunday when our family gets together, one person on all of our minds will be Alberto Torres, my late husband, who died 16 years ago on June 17, 1976. Easter Sunday would have marked his 66th birthday.

I am dedicating this column to him today. We met when I was 4 and he was 11. Our family, the Bustamantes, were the upstairs, next door neighbors. The Torreses were our *vecinos*. Alberto did not pay much attention to me when I was a little girl, or so I thought at the time. As years went by, it was more fun to be at the Torres's home than to be at ours because his sisters always had girls over to sing and talk about boys. They got to get dressed up and wear make-up. Also, it was fun to watch Albert make his balsa wood airplane models. It was also fun to see him keep his balance on "funny" skates. They had two little wooden balls, one in front and one in back, instead of four wheels. He loved his bike and did all kinds of maneuvers on it, even handstands, to impress me. And he did impress me. He always smiled. When I was very young, he taught me how to cross the street at Scott Avenue and 12th Street, where the corners come in irregularly. Later, he taught me how to ride my first two-wheeler. Later still, he taught me how to drive, and how to search the skies for the Big Dipper and the Little Dipper and other constellations. He watched out for me, always.

He had a bike paper route to help his mom, Teresita, who was a widow. During World War II, he went into the armed forces. His name was included on a large board inside the Cathedral St. Augustin, where all the Catholic kids in the armed forces had their names printed. Many parishioners not only prayed for their safe return but also lit candles at El Tiradito, the Wishing Shrine, asking for their safety. When a serviceman or woman died, we all knew it because a gold star was placed next to the deceased's name at church.

Thank God Albert never had a gold star. He did get tiny gold stars to show which battles he had fought in. Guadalcanal, Iwo Jima, and the Philippines (where he saw General MacArthur) are the ones I recall.

Albert never spoke about the war, except to say he would have liked to have seen the Philippines, which were so green, again. From Japan, he was sent home for his honorable discharge. We all celebrated. After that, he went to school on the G.I. Bill. He became an electrician journeyman and belonged to IBEW Local #570. Albert led an ordinary life, but to his family and friends, he was outstanding. We were wed at St. Philip's in the Hills on April 18, 1953. Our three children, Richard Michael, Albert Alexander and Esther Beya, and the other relatives remember him fondly. Albert never met his granddaughters, Shenoa, born two months after he died, and Jacquay, born two years later. Nor did he meet the grandson named after him.

They often hear us talk about Albert's ways. he was a most quiet, unassuming person. He communicated best playing flamencos, or classical pieces, on his *guitarra*. We loved to dance. He could transport me to Argentina with his tango. He never preached or told others how to be. He taught by example. He taught patience by being patient, consideration by being considerate, kindness by his kindness, unselfishness by being unselfish, and most of all, love by making others feel loved. He had a wonderful sense of humor. He was an old-fashioned gentle man. The best way to describe my Alberto is to say he was noble. In this way our grandson, Albert, reminds me of him, as do each of the rest of his heirs in other wonderful ways. I am truly grateful we shared life and family and friends, and good times and bad times.

Once the late Fred Acosta, who knew Albert well, told me how much he missed Albert's quiet strength. He said he drew strength from Albert. I thank God for Albert. He was my husband, but more than that, he was my best friend. May you also be blessed with many loving, beautiful, glorious memories and may you leave some for others. Happy Blessed, Holidays. *Cariñosamente, Alva.*

# Columnist Ties Up a Few Loose Ends

Writing my weekly column since August 1984 has been a wonderful experience for me. Hearing from you, my readers, has made it more enjoyable and worthwhile.

My primary employment is with Catholic Community Services in Project Ayuda, one of its numerous social service programs. I love it and it is rewarding. Like others, I am also involved with civic organizations, and enjoy volunteering—especially at St. Elizabeth of Hungary Clinic Auxiliary. The reason for all this explanation is so that you can understand why I have decided to soon discontinue writing my column. Although it's my choice to stop the column, it is still something akin to losing a friend. I will miss "talking" to you. But I need more time for my family and friends and also for myself. Before I say *adios*, I plan to write some recipes, those which have been requested most often. I am writing three short Mexican cookbooks. Each one will cover a specific time in the year. The first one will focus on Christmas holiday and its Mexican dishes and traditions. It should be ready to help with *nacimientos, empañadas, tamales, posadas, biscochuelos* and any other relevant information to give you a helping hand with the festivities. I'll let you know when it is ready.

Even though I am leaving the newspaper, it is my fervent hope that the column continues. In July, several people will be writing guest columns covering Mexican American cultural events and foods. *Hasta la vista.*

# Lorraine B. Aguilar a Blessing to Tucson

Lorraine Brichta Aguilar and I have been friends since we both attended first grade at Safford Elementary School.

The Brichta family, which consisted of mom Angelina and dad Albert, along with Norma, Albert, Betty and the youngest, Lorraine, lived across the street from St. Augustine Cathedral on South Stone Avenue. Next door was their Dad's service station, called Brichta's Standard/Chevron Station. Lorraine remembers:

FIGURE 9.3 Lorraine and Alva in 2010. Photo taken by Lydia R. Otero.

Every summer to keep cool, we slept in the side porch. We heard the church bells from early morning on through the day. Only after a while, I never even heard them anymore. They became a part of my life and so did the church. Lots of my friends feared Padre Pedro (P.P.) Timmerman, the pastor, but he was my friend and when Father Rosetti married us, on February 23, 1952, Rudy (her spouse) and I knelt before P.P. and he blessed us. Maybe that's why Rudy and I stayed together all these years—we had a special blessing. I had one of the safest and contented childhoods. I think I was born with a silver-plated spoon in my mouth. We were never rich, but I didn't know a need.

According to Lorraine her dad opened his service station at 7 a.m., then the family had lunch at noon and he took a siesta until 3. After his siesta, he kept the station open until the evening. It was when he took his siesta that she would go into the station and sell. She said:

We had the most beautiful array of penny candy. I sold that and I used to love to punch his cash register. I still recall a young customer who cheated us out of 5 cents.

Mother always took us downtown. That was our fun. We always bumped into people we knew. Mother would take us to Kress' five and ten-cent store and I remember running up and down the aisles. If you had a quarter to spend, you could buy a lot. I hate that there isn't a five-and-ten cent store any more.

I also remember the post office. We knew all the people. The Library Park was always safe. My Dad changed pay checks for SP (Southern Pacific) workers, and when I was between 10 and 12 he put up to $2,000 in a bag and I would go down to the bank and give the bag to the teller. How safe our streets were in the downtown area! I also remember the Old Pueblo Club was next to us and we knew it was an exclusive club.

I would go to church, in the month of May, every evening and offered cut flowers—if nothing else, poisonous oleanders. The girls and boys dressed all in white, the girls wore veils and offered flowers at church. The main song

FIGURE 9.4  Chevron Station on Stone Avenue in 1950s. Courtesy of Special Collections, University of Arizona Library.

we sang was the Hail Mary in Spanish to the Virgin. I remember my mother sending food to whomever was the pastor. If she made tamales or any special dishes, I was dancing across the street, taking him food. The priests were my friends. Mother had turkeys, chickens and doves. If the feathers grew too long, the turkeys flew over the fence. I recall chasing them down Stone [Avenue], in the center of town.

Lorraine has been an active participant in her children's education. She has been involved with education for 30 years. When the children began attending classes, she was an active PTA member. In 1979 she was appointed to monitor the implementation of the court desegregation in 20 schools in Tucson Unified School District, through an organization called IC— Independent Citizens. Next, she headed what was then called the Parents Partnership. For the first time this opened the door for representation of parents to appear before the school board at TUSD.

She also got to serve as one of two parents who were allowed to witness labor negotiations with the teachers' union and management. Lorraine also joined The Educational Enrichment Foundation, which helps raise funds and receives grants to give mini-grants to teachers and principals. The group has just received a grant from *Readers' Digest* of more than $1 million called "Library Power" for school libraries.

She has also served on the local Family Counseling Agency Board and with other civic and religious groups. In addition to all of this, she has been a giver to the community, in personal, warm ways, like baking countless, delicious *biscochuelos*—doughnut-like crunchy goodies—for every kind of charitable event, as well as for family, friends and neighbors' celebrations. She is a good cook. Her green corn tamales are legendary. In addition, for 12 years she has delivered meals to shut-ins via Mobile Meals.

Her most emphatic words were, "Every parent has to get and stay involved with their children and their education. That is the key. Then you see the difference. You get out of things only what you put into it." Lorraine has put in a lot. She is a great blessing to Tucson and to all who know her. She is a wonderful friend, a very special person, a joyous soul. She reminds me of an angel. I love her. *Hasta la vista.*

## We'll miss Alva Torres

We were sorry to read that Alva B. Torres has terminated her weekly column. Her articles regarding the locale, her family and friends, along with her gentle humor have been most interesting.

Life and history in the old Pueblo have brought back many memories. We also tried several of her recipes for that fabulous Mexican food. We will miss her and wish her the very best.

TOM & KATHERN JOHNSON

Editor's note: Although Alva B. Torres has retired, the Citizen is picking a replacement columnist we hope will be just as interesting.

FIGURE 9.5 Letter to the editor. *Citizen*, September 1, 1992, p. 7A.

# Tucson Grocery-store Treats Left Lasting, Sweet Memories

The word *"pilon"* lights up the eyes and brings a smile to the faces of Tucsonans who shopped for groceries here during the 1930s, 40s and in some cases early '50s.

Pilon, according to the Spanish dictionary, signifies gratuity or tax, but I am using this word the way we used it in Tucson. The Chinese and Mexican grocers gave their customers pilon as an appreciation for shopping with them. It was something sweet.

Our family used to shop first at Tang's Market and later at Jerry Lee Ho Market, on Saturdays. In those days, grocery shopping was a family affair, children accompanied their parents. For many, it was also the day to pay for the groceries families charged during the week. Most of all it was *el dia del pilon*, pilon day, with bags of sweets and sometimes even fruit.

One week we were expecting lots of relatives from both Mexico and California, and Mr. Lee gave us two huge, overflowing brown paper bags full of pilon. He included some special round cookies, dabbed with bright pink and white sparkling frosting. I can still see the bags, the familiar, friendly store and almost taste the wonderful cookies. That time our grocery bill must have been really big.

But getting back to the pilon itself, Joe Mendes, my compadre, says he recalls in the famous market San Juan de Letrán, in Mexico City, his sister having a food stall and giving away tiny *piloncillo* or brown sugar cones. These were given as pilon. We were thinking that maybe since piloncillos were given away, maybe north of the border the custom persisted but the word was shortened to pilon and included whatever sweet.

Aida Wilkins Mendes, my *comadre*, says that she cannot recall the name of the grocery store where she shopped, only that the owners were Chuck

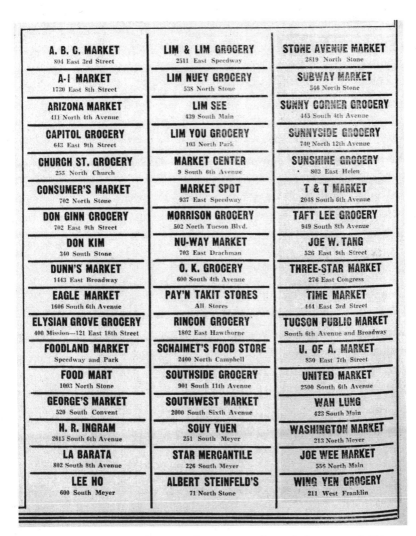

| A. B. C. MARKET | LIM & LIM GROCERY | STONE AVENUE MARKET |
|---|---|---|
| 804 East 3rd Street | 2511 East Speedway | 2819 North Stone |
| A-1 MARKET | LIM NUEY GROCERY | SUBWAY MARKET |
| 1730 East 8th Street | 538 North Stone | 546 North Stone |
| ARIZONA MARKET | LIM SEE | SUNNY CORNER GROCERY |
| 411 North 4th Avenue | 439 South Main | 445 South 4th Avenue |
| CAPITOL GROCERY | LIM YOU GROCERY | SUNNYSIDE GROCERY |
| 643 East 9th Street | 103 North Park | 740 North 12th Avenue |
| CHURCH ST. GROCERY | MARKET CENTER | SUNSHINE GROCERY |
| 255 North Church | 9 South 6th Avenue | • 803 East Helen |
| CONSUMER'S MARKET | MARKET SPOT | T & T MARKET |
| 702 North Stone | 937 East Speedway | 2048 South 6th Avenue |
| DON GINN GROCERY | MORRISON GROCERY | TAFT LEE GROCERY |
| 702 East 9th Street | 502 North Tucson Blvd. | 949 South 8th Avenue |
| DON KIM | NU-WAY MARKET | JOE W. TANG |
| 340 South Stone | 703 East Drachman | 526 East 9th Street |
| DUNN'S MARKET | O. K. GROCERY | THREE-STAR MARKET |
| 1443 East Broadway | 600 South 4th Avenue | 276 East Congress |
| EAGLE MARKET | PAY'N TAKIT STORES | TIME MARKET |
| 1606 South 6th Avenue | All Stores | 444 East 3rd Street |
| ELYSIAN GROVE GROCERY | RINCON GROCERY | TUCSON PUBLIC MARKET |
| 400 Mission—121 East 18th Street | 1802 East Hawthorne | South 6th Avenue and Broadway |
| FOODLAND MARKET | SCHAIMET'S FOOD STORE | U. OF A. MARKET |
| Speedway and Park | 2400 North Campbell | 850 East 7th Street |
| FOOD MART | SOUTHSIDE GROCERY | UNITED MARKET |
| 1003 North Stone | 901 South 11th Avenue | 2500 South 6th Avenue |
| GEORGE'S MARKET | SOUTHWEST MARKET | WAH LUNG |
| 520 South Convent | 2000 South Sixth Avenue | 423 South Main |
| H. R. INGRAM | SOUY YUEN | WASHINGTON MARKET |
| 2615 South 6th Avenue | 251 South Meyer | 213 North Meyer |
| LA BARATA | STAR MERCANTILE | JOE WEE MARKET |
| 802 South 8th Avenue | 226 South Meyer | 556 North Main |
| LEE HO | ALBERT STEINFELD'S | WING YEN GROCERY |
| 600 South Meyer | 71 North Stone | 211 West Franklin |

FIGURE 9.6 Advertisement that evidences a number of Chinese and Chinese American markets. *Arizona Daily Star*, March 3, 1939, p.10.

and Dave Fong and the store was at South Sixth Avenue and East 20th Street. "My husband, Joe, and I still run into Dave on our morning walks" and they remember pilon.

Genevieve Martinez Whalen was born at her home on the corner of Convento Avenue and Simpson Street, where her dad had the America Bakery.

That was its official name, but it was affectionately called *la tienda de Miguelito*, the store of her dad, Miguel. She remembers him giving *dulce y pan de huevo* (candy and a popular bun, topped with sugar and beaten egg yolks, especially tasty split, buttered and heated) as pilon.

Wanda Wong, whose dad, Johnny, owned the L&K Market, a name they inherited when they bought it, recalls that people charged their groceries, "They paid *cada quincena*, every 15 days, and when they did my dad handed out penny candy. On special occasions, he gave the kids ice cream bars," I interjected, had I known would have gladly walked to that Riverside market. I never even tasted an ice cream bar in those days. Wanda continued, "Dad also gave one-half gallon ice cream blocks around the holidays and to couple of good customers he sometimes gave a quart of beer." That was a very rare pilon.

Another grocery store, Don Watt's, was also on Riverside, and that is where Soila Bernardina Gracia's (now Celaya) family shopped, "I remember looking forward to the day my dad would go and pay on the bill and then, *aquí viene el pilon*—here comes the pilon. It was a treat because our parents did not buy us candy. Even mom would use it to make us behave. '*Pórtense bien por que hoy veine el pilon*,' behave well because today comes the pilon. I remember candy that looked like little ice cream cones," she continued, as she held up her index finger and thumb to show about one to two inches. "Ay, they were so pretty." she smiled longingly.

Pilon made our lives sweeter. Next week we will continue with more on pilon. Do you know anyone who still gives pilon? If so, let me know ASAP. *Hasta la vista.*

# *Pilon* was Much Better Than Grocery Coupons

To continue last week's column on *pilon*: This was the name given to the commodities that Chinese and Mexican grocery merchants gave their customers for shopping with them. A little appreciation you could eat or drink.

Actually, I like it better than discount coupons, which just take more paper and therefore knock down more trees. It would be nice if the manufacturers would simply lower the prices and the stores would give pilon.

Sally Yanez said that her family shopped at Jerry Lee Ho's and that he was very generous. "I used to love the gingersnaps, that's what I remember, those gingersnaps which we received in our pilon, along with candy."

Delicia Miranda Reynolds happily recounted her experiences She said, "We lived on 24th Street and there was this little grocery store on the corner of 23rd and South Sixth Avenue where the Pep Boys is now. Lee Lok (the proprietor), gave us pilon, regardless of whether I went with one of my sisters, Sofie, Evelina, Elva or Norma, and bought one article or bags full when we went on the weekends with our parents, Alfredo and Petrocinia. Then we got bags of pilon including fruit."

Ofelia Vargas, who lived in Morenci, says the Mexican merchants gave penny gum in that town, and that the customers appreciated it. Amelia Leon gave me this information: "The last time I got pilon was on Meyer Avenue at Del Monte Market from Henry and Frank Gee. I was 9. We shopped every two weeks so you can imagine how much pilon we received—candy cookies and fruit."

Señor Salvador Galvan, who grew up in Mexico says, "*Era atracción para atraer a los chamacos* (It was to attract the kids). When my mother would ask me to go to nearby grocery store, I would reply, no mama. That was because they did not give pilon there." He explained he was willing to go further if necessary to wherever they gave pilon. "They had to give pilon, because those that did not, their business went down," he laughed.

Esther Tang, who speaks English, Spanish and a Chinese dialect, as did all Chinese merchants and their children in the days of pilon, mentioned a commodity given as pilon which was unique, I think. Esther's dad, Don Wah, and his family lived in the area now known as La Placita and they had their own grocery store, but no meat department. So, they bought their meat from Louis Peyron, the butcher who had a meat market on Convent Avenue. Since they were used to pilon being given out by their dad, they expected and always asked Peyron, "Louis, where's our pilon?" Whereupon Mr. Peyron would hand them a wiener or two.

Esther also says that she and her husband had Dave's One Stop on 29th Street and 6th Avenue, and that even in the 50's, they continued to give their good customers pilon. She also mentioned how trusting people were. When their customers charged food, her mother would note it by item on a little wallet sized notebook, which she handed to the customers. On payday, they would hand it back to her and she would total it up and they would pay. Then she would tear out the charges and hand them the book back, which they used the following week. No other accounting method was kept.

Our neighbors, which later became family, shopped on the corner of Cushing Street and South 6th Avenue at a store called Don Kims. They carried fresh poultry and gave good pilon also. But what I recall most about that store was the fancy and modern multicolored neon chicken on top of the store. It appeared to move its little chicken feet. Watching that magic on a summer evening with both the electric running chicken and the stars shining overhead and piece of candy from pilon was a wonderful time. Now all those happy, giving and sharing days are pilon to the spirit. I hope somebody gives you pilon too. *Hasta la vista.*

# Radio Pioneer had a Positive Impact

For Thanksgiving I thank God for all the times I have had the privilege of writing to and for all of you. I also want you to pardon me for the long delays in answering my mail. Some have asked me when my cookbook is coming out and I have not been able to answer you because I really do not know. Whenever it does, I will have it publicized some way or another.

Leaving the column is not easy, because I really enjoy writing and communicating with you, and sharing my stories and recipes with you. I know I will miss you. My parents' health is frail. I want to give them more time now. That is the main reason for discontinuing my column.* My last regular column is slated for New Year's Day. Hopefully, we can still be in touch once in a while, as I submit guest columns in the coming years and share new recipes or new ways of preparing them.

Another thank you today goes to a special group of people who have made an exceptionally important and unique impact in our area, particularly and most directly to our Spanish-speaking community: our Spanish-speaking radio station managers and their entire staffs. In Tucson we have KTZR (1450 AM), Radio Pantera; KXEW (1600 AM), Radio Fiesta; and KQTL (1210 AM), Radio Que Tal, as well as a new bilingual station KOHT (98.3 FM) with 10,000 watts that reaches seven counties, as well as northern Mexico.

I was able to interview three people affiliated with KQTL so that you might get a feel for the contributions this medium has made, and continues to make, in our Hispanic community. Before that, I need to mention Don Jacinto Orozco, Tucson's first Spanish-speaking announcer, the pioneer in

---

*Alva's father Miguel died December 17, 1993 and her mother Carmen died less than two weeks later on January 5, 1994.

FIGURE 9.7 Jacinto Orozco (wearing a traditional charro sombrero) headlining a promotional event in 1946 at the Plaza Market that once stood at 112 West Broadway. Courtesy of Raymond R. Orozco.

this field. Shortly after arriving in Tucson in 1938 from Jerome, Arizona, he started his early morning programs at 4 a.m., and continued for three hours. That was the time that was available, and it was a good time because all the miners and other workers had an opportunity to listen to him while getting ready or while on their way to work. Children could also listen to an afternoon program.

Every time Julietita, my little sister, and I heard his lively theme song "Las Zacatecas," we immediately ran around our home like galloping cowgirls, being both pony and rider, slapping our backsides joyfully as we pranced, as children do. Even now, as an *abuelita*, I must confess I still gallop once in a while, or at least dance when I hear that song and I always recall those days with happiness.

Don Jacinto was the one communicator who not only told us the news but just as importantly announced all social events. When he played a song, it was inevitably "under" a myriad of names. Dedications were mostly for birthdays and Saints' Days. If we were lucky we could hear about half of the song without *dedicaciones*. But that did not bother us, we accepted it because now we knew which friends were celebrating. There were special dedications for newborns, *primera comuniones* (First Communions), graduating students, welcoming visitors to town, as well as family and friends departing and anniversaries. This was usually also where we heard the burial arrangements, as well as the appointed time and date for rosaries and wakes. Without Don Jacinto we would not have been such a close community. He, like present day radio personnel, got involved with charitable fund-raisers.

When he died in 1971, the Yaqui (Yoeme) Indians held a special all-night wake for him. Only Yaquis attended. The next day Don Jacinto lay in his coffin in a charro outfit with a big, beautiful charro hat on the lid, and when the mariachis played "Las Zacatecas" at his funeral mass at La Catedral San Augustin, there wasn't a dry eye to be seen anywhere. We loved him and think of him fondly.

To be continued next week. *Hasta la vista.*

# Spanish Stations Ride the Radio Waves

I reiterate what I said last week. Thank you, Lord, for the privilege of writing this column for all of my readers. It has given me immeasurable pleasure to share recipes, stories and memories, and to introduce a few of the people who have contributed to our wonderful town.

Last week I told you about Don Jacinto Orozco, our pioneer in Spanish-language radio, who was the main communicator in the Mexican American population and who worked as a radio announcer with a lot of *gusto* for 33 years. Today I continue with interviews of three people directly involved in the same medium, at radio KQTL. The call letters translate when spoken into *que tal?* which means, "How are you? How goes it?"

First, I spoke to Ernesto Portillo Sr., who is the national and regional sales-man as well as the president of the corporation. His radio career began at age 17 with a job as a disc jockey in Juarez, Chihuahua, Mexico. He shared that:

In 1954 I was invited to join in the then—new KEVT. I came and fell in love with Tucson, and its people. I stayed with that station till 1960. That year I went to work for a life insurance company. In 1963, I joined the soon-to-be-born KXEW. I was sales manager and six months later, I took over as manager of the station. A few years later, a group of Tucsonans and I bought the station, which we operated until 1981. That year it was sold. For 25 years, I remained as a consultant.

In 1985 members of El Sahuarito Broadcasting Co. invited me to join their corporation and to build and operate KQTL It opened on October 12 of that year. The broadcasting facility is on the Old Nogales Highway and new studios and offices are at 2955 East Broadway. As of 2½ years ago, Raul Gámez Bogarin took over as station manager. He enjoys his job because it's people-oriented . . .

We try to touch people on a daily basis in all aspects—religious, socially, politically, economically and personally—total community involvement.

Next, I spoke to Claudio Jimenez y Fernandez. He was born in Xalapa, Veracruz, Mexico. His first visit to Tucson was in 1956, when he met Lorenzo Palma, a well-known Spanish speaking radio announcer, now deceased, at El Casino Ballroom. In 1958 he took a vacation in Mexico City and there met Arturo Aguilar, the manager of KEVT. He invited him to come to Tucson and join the station. Jimenez began to work at the station on February 1, 1959. He became program director and stayed until 1967. "Then I went with KXEW as radio announcer and newscaster. I stayed there until January 31, 1980." In 1981 he joined Tucson Unified School District as its first translator, while still translating news for KXEW. He left the district in 1987. In 1988, back at KXEW, he returned to the program *La Palabra del Dia* (LPdD), the word for today. In 1992 he joined radio KQTL with his program LPdD, and *La Hora del Cafe*. On LPdD Jimenez takes a word and gives the meaning and pronounces it several times so that people can learn it that day. And *La Hora del Cafe* is an informal coffee hour when he interviews people and talks with them about their concerns.

Raúl Gamez Bogarin was born in Cananea, Sonora, Mexico (Amazingly, according to Isidro Figueroa, 218 residents of this mining town became radio announcers.) Said Bogarin:

Since I was a little child I listened to the radio and I liked it so much that I began to participate as I progressed in school, as an orator and in poetry *declamaciónes*. In 1960 I arrived in Tucson and attended Pueblo High School. In order to support myself I worked at La Fiesta Drive-In Theater, the only drive-in that showed Hispanic movies. I worked in the snack bar. I met Gaston Galaz, who was in the National Guard who introduced me to Ernesto Portillo. They opened the door for me to start at KEVT. At that time, it was on only from sunrise to sunset. I was 17 at the time and was the youngest announcer. At first, I took care of the record library and then they allowed me to record public service announcements and finally commercials. I used to run from school to catch the bus on the Old Pueblo Laos bus line. I got out at 3:45 and arrived running at 4:30 p.m., just in time to go on the air. It was quite an experience. I had the privilege of working with some of the best Spanish speaking radio announcers in Tucson: Ernesto Portillo, Lorenzo Palma, Claudio Jimenez, Henry Villegas, Marcos Garcia Ayala, Ismael Ortega, Manuel Palma Parra and Arnulfo "Fito" Palma, and because of that I was able to learn radio announcing. I had good models and tremendous acceptance. Because of the tone of my voice people thought I was older than I was. When I was introduced, they were surprised.

I never left Tucson, as I had initially intended. Ever since then I have been involved with communication—radio, TV, and newspapers. I have been involved with bilingual advertising and public relations. The latest experience I had was when I joined cable TV. So, I have been in every aspect. As general manager I feel we have a tremendous obligation. Our radio KQTL has 10,000 watts capacity and reaches all of southern Arizona. We are in a position to be a voice of the Hispanics in the whole region, not just in communication. Our responsibility is to be a source of information to our Hispanic population and we have an educational and a civic responsibility.

These men have all been involved, along with other men and women in the media, particularly Bertha Gallegos, with many civic and individual fundraisers. They made a huge impact while the amnesty provisions of the 1986 Immigration Reform and Control Act were in effect. They held a radio-thon a few days before the deadline for registration, helping raise $20,000 for those who sought legal residence, but had no means of coming up with the immigration fees. We know that our Spanish-speaking radio announcers and personnel have been the thread of communication which runs through the fabric of our Hispanic community, holding it together. More than that, they helped design the pattern.

*MUCHISIMAS GRACIAS a todos ustedes. Queridos* readers, Happy Thanksgiving. *Hasta la vista.*

# 1993

# Hasta la vista

*Citizen Editor's: Alva Torres doesn't like to say goodbye, and we hate to see her go. But Torres, a Tucson Citizen columnist since 1984, will step down as a regular columnist to write a book, take care of her family and pursue other projects. She'll appear from time to time in these pages.*

\* \* \*

Dearest readers, it's not easy to say adios, es *muy, muy, difícil.*

Still, I am grateful for the wonderful opportunity that was given to me by the Citizen during the summer of 1984 when my columns began with the recipe for *chiles rellenos*, my favorite Mexican dish. The column began strictly as a recipe column on Mexican food, and eventually evolved into a column on early Tucson Mexican culture, people who were and are important to this Old Pueblo. And then, finally, I wrote about all kinds of lovely people and events and remembrances. It has been such a privilege to get to better know those I interviewed. It has been so much fun to "talk" to you, dear readers.

Thank goodness we have a fine, professional writer, Carmen Villa Prezelski, taking over the column. I have greatly enjoyed reading her articles, as well as Alice Meza's and those of other guests. Once in a while, I'll make a guest appearance. That makes it easier to leave.

A number of people have written and others have asked me why I am leaving, so it is fair to tell you that the main reason is because of my mother's frail health. And if any of you

### TUESDAY

## Adios, Alva: We'll miss your column

Alva Torres writes her last regularly scheduled Tucson Citizen column tomorrow — but she'll still visit. Meanwhile, she wants to wish you all well. See tomorrow's Citizen.

FIGURE 10.1 Announcement. *Citizen,* January 4, 1993, p. 1B.

know her, we would greatly appreciate hearing from you soon, while she can still recall you. You may contact her by calling 624-XXXX. Both she and my father would love to hear from you.

This year, we began celebrating the holidays with a wonderful Hanukkah dinner at the home of my sister, Esther Jacobson, and her husband, Stan. The home, decorated in gold and shimmering blue, was a sight to behold. The menorah was lit, and Stan sang the proper holy days prayers. They used china from both sides of the family. Stan made the best smoked turkey, followed by delicious salads and a lot of other goodies, including espresso and Hungarian apple pie. Everything at that home is kosher.

All of this took me back to our own holiday celebrations, which we joyously celebrated when I lived as a child on McCormick Street. Then, as now, the main thing was the love we all shared. That was the foundation of our Christmas. You could feel it all around as we continued our celebration on Christmas Eve at the home of my other sister, Julieta, and her husband, Ernesto Portillo. It was particularly touching when they opened their gift from their children. It was presented with aplomb and joy and cleverly done. The gift itself was a wrought-iron fence with an arch proclaiming "Casita Portillo," for their little house in Patagonia. It was done by presenting parts of the old fence and before-and-after photos, including those of the work in progress. The whole family formed a loving circle, including the latest addition, Mario Rene Portillo, born August 24. What joy for all of us. Christmas Day was at our home, with all of us: Wilma and Rudy Soto, my family's in-laws and our Nani.

To launch this new year, remember that nothing is more important than our own attitude and what we bring to the moment by our thoughts. In the Bible, in the book of Philippians, we are told: "Whatsoever things are true, whatsoever things are honest, whatsoever things are just, whatsoever things are pure, whatsoever things are lovely, whatsoever things are good report, if there be any virtue and if there be any praise, think on these things . . . and the God of peace shall be with you." May God keep in his bosom all of our loved ones who departed last year. God bless all of us with grace. May this year be the very best you can make it, in the spirit of love.

*Cariñosamente*, Alva.

# Epilogue

The *Citizen* invited a few columnists to fill in for Alva B. Torres once she announced her departure. *Tucsonenses* Alicia Meza, Velia Morelos and Carmen Villa Prezelski stepped in and contributed a few columns. After some deliberation, the *Citizen* selected Prezelski to replace Torres. Her first column, "She's Josie—or Carmen—Depending on When You Met," appeared on December 29, 1992. Carmen Villa Prezelski contributed a weekly column to the *Citizen* for the next fourteen years. Her last column appeared on March 24, 2006. The *Citizen*, "the oldest continuously published newspaper in Arizona," a casualty of declining subscriptions and sales, ceased publishing its newspaper in 2009.

Alva B. Torres would write an occasional column for the paper for the next few years after resigning her column. As of 2021, 89-year-old Alva lives in Tucson with her daughter Esther. She remains close to her family and large network of friends. She is also active in a few community organizations.

FIGURE 11.1 Alva continues to share her perspectives and opinions at a 2017 community event. Courtesy Joseph "Bob" Diaz.

# Recipes

The following recipes were a part of one of the earlier columns, or included because of their local appeal.

## January 30, 1985
### Simple Dessert Recalls Simpler Days

Some like it hot, some like it cold, but it won't last nine days. What are we talking about? An old-time favorite dessert, *arroz con leche* (Rice with Milk).

Teresita Torres [mother-in-law], whom we all call Nani or Mrs. T., was born in 1898 on a ranch outside of Tucson. She has good recollection of the Old Pueblo when she was growing up here. At one time, she lived in the old Fremont House. At that time, Leopoldo Carrillo was the owner, and he owned more homes than anyone else around, Mrs. T. recalls the *Papagas* (Tohono O'Odham women)* balancing *ollas* (jugs) on their heads. Inside the ollas were the different foods that they sold.

One of the things Mrs. T's mother used to cook back then was a simple dessert, made with rice and milk, called arroz con leche. Here is Nani's recipe from before the time that Congress Street, which she still calls *Congreso*, had wooden planks for sidewalks and when proper respect was shown to your mother by kneeling as you handed her a plate of arroz con leche.

ARROZ CON LECHE
   2½ cups of milk
   ½ cup of rice

---

*The tribe voted to officially change their name to Tohono O'Odham in 1986.

2 to 4 tablespoons of sugar

1 to 2 cinnamon sticks

1 egg

½ teaspoon of vanilla

A dash of cinnamon powder

1. Place milk, rice, first sugar and cinnamon in a heavy pan.

2. Bring all of the ingredients to a boil. You must watch it carefully because it can spill over in the twinkling of an eye and make a big mess.

3. Lower the flame to a slow simmer and cover with a tight-fitting lid.

4. Continue to simmer until the rice is tender, about 40 to 50 minutes. If necessary add more milk. Do Not Stir.

5. When it is just about ready, separate the egg white from the yolk.

6. Beat the white until it is a thick froth; then add the second sugar and vanilla.

7. Continue to whip as you add the yolk.

8. Next take a bit of the cooked rice and stir it into the whipped-egg mixture.

9. Then gently fold all of this into the rest of the cooked rice.

10. Serve it warm, generously sprinkling it with cinnamon powder.

Some people like it served cold. A few old-timers make it with condensed milk and water.

Nani says that when nothing was available, they still made it with water in the place of milk. Many people like to cook it with raisins or else they add some when it is served. Either way, it still is called arroz con leche.

Another version that might appeal to you and your family is one that I concocted for the new style of eating:

## NEW-STYLE ARROZ CON LECHE

2½ cups of low-fat milk

½ cup of quick brown rice

2 tablespoons of brown sugar

2 tablespoons of pecans

1 egg

½ teaspoon of ground nutmeg

A dash of ground nutmeg and ground pecans

Follow the same recipe as you did for the regular Arroz con leche, but substituting these ingredients. Nani says she likes them both. After all, staying young is all in your attitude, as we all know. Trying new foods or new recipes is one easy way to do this.

## July 15, 1986
### Simple Salsa

A good old recipe from those days is a very simple salsa, which is a good accompaniment for broiled or charcoaled ribs. When you are cooking the ribs, add to the grill whole fresh tomatoes and whole stalks of green onions and fresh Anaheim chiles. Blister all and place the chiles in a brown paper bag to "sweat." Doing this makes it very easy to peel the chiles. Be sure to remove the seeds also. Then slice the chiles and onions and crush the tomatoes. Add garlic and fresh cilantro, sliced along with a bit of crushed oregano. Place all of these into a glass container and add a dash of vinegar and a tablespoon or so of olive oil. Serve with ribs, potato salad and the ever-present tortillas and frijoles. Iced lemonade or tea makes it perfect.

## April 25, 1989
### Mexican Drinks are Cool, Refreshing Treat

If you've been to some of the Mexican fiestas held annually in Tucson, you've seen many different kinds of drinks. One of the most popular is *horchata*, a drink made from rice. Other very popular drinks include agua de melon, tepache and *teswin*, as well as *aguas de jicama, de jamaica, de pina, de manzana* and *de limon*.

Following are recipes for horchata, tepache and teswin.

### HORCHATA
3 cups of white rice

4 cups of sugar

1 can of evaporated milk

2 tablespoons of vanilla

cinnamon powder to suit

1 gallon of water

1. Soak the rice overnight in enough water for all the rice to expand. (Packages of crushed rice are available in Nogales, Sonora, at most markets if you do not want to go to the trouble of crushing the soaked rice in the blender.)

2. Divide the rice into small batches, then place batches in blender and blend into a paste. You might need to add more water as you are doing this.

3. Mix the rice and the remaining ingredients with the water, stirring until the sugar is dissolved.

4. Refrigerate in a covered glass or plastic container, so that it does not pick up any metallic or refrigerator taste.

6. Serve chilled with plenty of crushed ice or ice cubes, being sure to stir before serving, as the rice tends to settle.

The *agua de melon* follows the same recipe as the horchata, but use crushed melon seeds instead of rice and pass the drink through a colander before serving. In this part of the country teswin is the name given to the pineapple drink, but in some parts of Mexico that is called *tepache*.

## TEPACHE

peelings of 1 pineapple

3 panochas (Mexican brown sugar cones) of medium size

cinnamon to suit

1 teaspoon of cloves

1. Place the pineapple peelings with two panochas and the rest of the ingredients in a glass or ceramic-covered container.

2. Let this ferment for four days, then remove 1 cups of the liquid and add the third panocha.

3. Ferment covered for another 9 days in a cool, dark area.

4. It has a kick and you should not keep it longer. If you do, be sure to refrigerate it and drink it fairly soon. Always served with plenty of ice.

The third recipe is really better made with panocha, which is available in many of the stores on the west and south sides of Tucson. If this is too much trouble or not possible, substitute 3/4 cup brown sugar per panocha (more if you love things very sweet). You can always adjust the amount to suit your taste.

## TESWIN
    1 package of pinole
    1 cinnamon stick
    3 panochas
    1 gallon of water

    1. Place all of the ingredients in a glass container, covered.
    2. Serve with crushed ice. This has to be stirred even when drinking as the pinole quickly settles to the bottom.

Pinole is made of crushed maize and crushed wheat and is available in specialty stores where Mexican food is sold. I remember as a child just stirring pinole into a cold glass of milk, adding sugar by the tablespoon and sprinkling it with cinnamon powder. It is an easy and nourishing drink for everyone. I can provide recipes of those other Mexican drinks if you are interested. Let me know and I will include them in a future column. *Hasta la vista.*

# September 4, 1990
## Try Verdolagas for a Late-Summer Salad

I hope all of you had a wonderful Labor Day and are ready to get to work again. Since summer weather will still be with us for a while and summer harvest is in full swing, I would like to publish a variation of recipes for verdolagas.

Verdolagas grows wild, like weeds. But they are far from weeds. They make a very tasty vegetable side or main dish and they also make a refreshing salad. Before cooking or eating them, be sure you have verdolagas and not *cochitos*, a weed that resembles verdolagas. Cochitos have bigger and fatter leaves and stems. Verdolagas are tender, have small leaves and grow in many of the yards, gardens and vacant lots in the old parts of town.

## BASIC VERDOLAGAS

1–2 pounds of thoroughly washed and drained verdolagas
1 small onion finely sliced
1 medium tomato, diced
¼ to 1 pound of yellow or white cheese that melts, sliced
salt or suitable substitute to taste

1. Sauté the onion and tomato till limp
2. Add the verdolagas and cook till totally limp, then add the cheese and lower the flame so the cheese melts. Add salt to suit.
3. Cover and let the flavor blend. Serve with flour tortillas.


When you pick the verdolagas, rinse them thoroughly. If you are not going to cook them right away, place them in a plastic bag and refrigerate. They do not keep long but the above recipe only takes a few minutes.

Depending on the amount of cheese you add, it can be either a side or main dish. Other variations include adding sliced green onion, peeled green chiles and a little milk. Another variation is to make a salad. Here's a variation from Amelia Leon: She chops the verdolagas and adds minced onion and diced tomatoes, finely minced chili jalapeno with a dash of vinegar and oil. She serves this cold.

# September 4, 1990
## Leche Quemada

In response to the reader who wrote about the Leche Quemada, you are correct: It never will thicken to the consistency of fudge, in fact it will not thicken at all. I remember Mama often making Leche Quemada with a can of Eagle Brand sweetened condensed milk. She would place this can in a large pot of water and bring it to a rolling boil and then she would lower the flame to a simmer and cook it for hours and hours. When she turned it off, she would leave it in the pot, water and all, until it was completely cool and then she opened the can and poured out the Leche Quemada. We would spread it on bread.

# February 5, 1991

One dish Margret Torres Donsky [sister-in-law] cooked before she married and which she taught me was one which had been handed down to her by her father, Arturo, so that is what we call it. It had been given to him by an Italian friend.

### ARTURO'S SPAGHETTI SAUCE
4 tablespoons of good olive oil
3 cups of sliced onions
a clove of minced garlic
1 pound of fresh tomatoes
¼ cup of chile paste
1 teaspoon each of celery salt and dry mustard
½ to 1 teaspoon of ground cloves
1 cup of sliced mushrooms
1 pound of diced ham

1. Sauté the onions and garlic in the olive oil until wilted.
2. In a pan brown the diced ham.
3. Add all the ingredients together and simmer for hours.
4. Immediately before serving. over spaghetti, add peas. An option is to add green olives.

# June 25, 1991

Here's a nice recipe that came to our family through my dear grandmother, Mama Bella. She called it *Guisado de la Plaza*. It tastes best if you buy a large rolled roast and use the leftover portion to make this nice summer dish.

### GUISADO DE LA PLAZA
4 cups of cooked roast, diced into ½-inch pieces
2 cups parboiled potatoes, diced ¼-inch
Half of a thinly sliced cabbage
1 small can of tomato sauce, diluted and seasoned
1 small white onion, thinly sliced
Parmesan cheese

1. Cook the roast, first inserting a number of garlic cloves into the meat. The roast should be cooked and cooled.

2. Then take the parboiled diced potatoes and sauté them in your favorite cooking oil, toasting them lightly. Then do the same with the meat.

3. Meanwhile, slice the cabbage and keep it cold.

4. To prepare the sauce, dilute the tomato sauce with about a half a can of water, depending on your taste, and then add a few dashes of good wine vinegar, oregano to suit and plenty of garlic salt. Let this sit for a while. In fact, it's better to make it a day ahead, cover it tightly and refrigerate.

5. To serve the guisado, place the mixture of potatoes and meat on the serving plate, top with the cold cabbage and douse liberally with the sauce. On top of this, place the thinly sliced onions and sprinkle with cheese. Serve with homemade corn tortillas, if possible, or store-bought ones. A nice glass of cool beverage with a light dessert and you have an enjoyable summer dinner.

# April 7, 1992

A popular Lenten dessert, the following easy recipe is from the Carrillo School cookbook.

### CAPIROTADA OR BREAD PUDDING

12 slices of toasted bread
1 cup of raisins
2 cups of grated cheese
½ cup of chopped cilantro
Peanut butter to spread on the toasted bread (consistency to suit).
The syrup needs to be prepared separately and integrated before
   cooking.
### SYRUP
3 panochas (Mexican brown sugar cones)
½ cup maple syrup
3 or 4 green onions,
3 cups of water
1 cinnamon stick

1. Boil these ingredients and then remove the onion. (This is optional, but if you leave it in, cut it into bite sizes.)

2. In a baking dish, set a layer of bread, already spread with the peanut butter. Sprinkle cheese, raisins and cilantro, then pour syrup over all. Continue to layer and cover with syrup until it is soaked through, making sure you top if off with the cheese. Place in the oven set at 350 degrees for about half an hour, or until the cheese is well-melted.

3. As far as the cheese, any good melting white or yellow is fine. This is another variation of the basic recipe. That one calls for Spanish peanuts, in place of the peanut butter. The taste is still unique for a bread pudding. Some people add more cheese and cut down on the bread. Variations include using apples and prunes as well as bananas along with the raisins. Nuts other than peanuts sometimes get in there and I have tasted it made with corn tortillas and apricots or canned fruit cocktail. What is important is the essence of the cilantro, the *cebollita verde* (green onion) and the cheese mixture.

# Acknowledgements

Special thanks to Esther Torres who worked closely with her mother Alva to identify the approximate date and the people in their family photographs. Raymond R. Orozco and Irma Moreno generously allowed the publication of their photographs in *Notitas*. Joseph "Bob" Diaz at Special Collections at the University of Arizona was critical as deadlines approached and saved the day by expediting permissions and photos for this book. Patricia Ballesteros also stepped in to ensure some key photographs were included in *Notitas*. Theater maker Marc David Pinate, the Producing Director at Borderlands helped launch this book in its earlier stages and also deserves many, many thanks.